Camino de santiago

Camino de Santiago
Fingerprints of God

Paul Moylan

TATE PUBLISHING & *Enterprises*

Camino de Santiago
Copyright © 2011 by Paul Moylan. All rights reserved.

No part of this publication may be reproduced, stored in a retrieval system or transmitted in any way by any means, electronic, mechanical, photocopy, recording or otherwise without the prior permission of the author except as provided by USA copyright law.

The opinions expressed by the author are not necessarily those of Tate Publishing, LLC.

Published by Tate Publishing & Enterprises, LLC
127 E. Trade Center Terrace | Mustang, Oklahoma 73064 USA
1.888.361.9473 | www.tatepublishing.com

Tate Publishing is committed to excellence in the publishing industry. The company reflects the philosophy established by the founders, based on Psalm 68:11,
"The Lord gave the word and great was the company of those who published it."

Book design copyright © 2011 by Tate Publishing, LLC. All rights reserved.
Cover design by Blake Brasor
Interior design by Lindsay B. Behrens

Published in the United States of America
ISBN: 978-1-61777-203-0
1. Travel / Europe / Spain   2. Travel / Hikes & Walks
11.10.06

*To my wife Sandra,
my mother & father Moira & Finlay,
and my brothers and sisters,
Philip, Marie, Jacinta, Theresa, Patricia, Eileen and Brian.*

Acknowledgements

I've never written an acknowledgement before this one. As I consider what the words should be, I realize the list of people to thank is longer than I can begin to appreciate.

My wife, Sandra, has been my love, my partner, my support, my inspiration, my challenger, and my cheerleader for this book, on my *Camino* journeys, and in my life. We both read the original articles that started me on the walks, and without her equal passion and support, I'm not sure I would have done the first trip.

My father, Finlay, who died of Alzheimer's complications in 1997, and my mother, Moira, who turns ninety this year, dedicated everything, their entire lives, to raising their children as best they could. They provided a happy home, unconditional love, the finest possible example of faith, and unwavering support through good times and tribulation. My brothers and sisters follow in the model my parents set out, loving and supporting me in ways I can't do justice to here. To be born into so much love has been one of the greatest gifts of my life.

The men of what I call my breakfast club have been an inspiration to the process of this book and on my journeys of the *Camino*. Barry, Eric, Gerry, Marc, the two Mikes, Jerome, and Terry are both friends and models of how to do life—strong and humble, spiritual, caring and welcoming, accepting struggles and reward equally as they journey. I should do so well. I need to offer a special thank you to Michael Froh from this group, who gave his time to review several versions on my manuscript. His insights, personal spirituality and gentle guiding hand contributed substantially to the end result of my book.

I have met amazing people of faith in my life, perhaps none more inspirational than Father Joe LeClair. He has been a pastor and friend for over fifteen years and instrumental in subtle and not-so-subtle ways in how my *Camino* walk unfolded. For that, I owe a great debt.

Caroline became important in my life when I needed to accept and move beyond my own limitations. Her knowledge, wisdom, strength, and guidance lifted me up, and I'm not sure this book would have happened without her.

Friends have been many, and again, I've been blessed to call them that. At the risk of missing some who helped shape my life, I'll resist more names. All have contributed in no small part to who I am today. The path ahead is not without rocks and stones. But if I remember to appreciate the love in my life and look up every now to say thank you, it's a spectacular journey.

Foreword:
The Camino de Santiago

The Camino de Santiago, or The Way of St. James as it's known in English, is a month long walk via an ancient pilgrimage trail. It spans the distance across northern Spain, from the Pyrenees Mountains in the east, to the city of Santiago de Compostela in the north western corner of the Iberian Peninsula. The walk dates to the 9th century, when the tomb of the apostle James, who had originally evangelized Spain, was discovered near Compostela. The modern day Spanish Tourist Board identifies the Emperor Charlemagne as first to make the sojourn across the country to venerate the tomb of the apostle shortly after its discovery. This and a similar journey by a local bishop around the same time period are credited as instigating the Camino as a Christian pilgrimage. As the news of the tomb spread across Europe, people began to follow the footsteps of these original two, making the journey across Spain on foot as a pilgrimage to St. James.

History suggests millions made the journey during the 700 years that followed the initial discovery of the apostle's remains. Interest waned in the 16th century, though it never completely died off, and for reasons not entirely clear, then began recovering in the late 20th century. The popularity of the Camino has since been boosted by publicity surrounding two visits from Pope John Paul II, and another more recently by Pope Benedict the XVI. The trail to Santiago de Compostela received further notoriety when it was also declared a **UNESCO** World heritage site in 1993.

Over the last three decades, the annual number walking the 500-mile trail has grown exponentially. At the outset of the 1980s, trekkers numbered a few thousand annually. By the middle of the next decade, the yearly number had grown to some 20,000. In 2003 when I walked, 75,000 made the journey with me during that year. In 2010, over a quarter of a million walkers from literally all over the world made the journey. The numbers speak to the growth phenomenon of the Camino, as do the growing number of Internet forums on the subject.

It takes about a month to walk the 1,200 year old footpath. Carrying only the essentials in a backpack, walkers set out, most on their own or with a friend or two, and head out across mountain and plain for reasons often unclear. They describe a sense of simply being drawn to Spain upon hearing of the pilgrimage trail, and its history.

Overnight accommodations are via a Spanish style of bunkhouse known as refugios, these costing less than ten dollars a night. For Americans, Canadians, Europeans, Australians, New Zealanders, South Americans and people from dozens of other countries who have done the walk, the overnight stops are a fascinating part of the journey. The modern day pilgrims trek from the French-Spanish border, completing their trek at the Cathedral of Santiago in the city of Santiago de Compostela, where a crypt below the alter is said to still house the remains of St. James.

The great majority who do walk are not long distance hikers, marathoners or other hyper sports people. Most are average people, drawn to spend a month away from technology and the busyness of life, to discover what the Camino holds for them. Most return describing their walk as peaceful, meditative, and transformative, calling it the journey of a lifetime. It is this word of mouth about such deeply personal experiences that has spawned the rapid growth of modern day pilgrims.

Table of Contents

Small Questions 15
The Large Question 17
Out of the Closet 23

The 2003 Walk 37
   Five Letters, a Prophet, and a Shepherd. 39
      September 2, 2003. 45
      September 11, 2003. 57
      September 18, 2003. 70
      September 23, 2003. 82
      October 1, 2003. 91

The Second Camino 125
   The Path Back to Spain 127
      Four Days to Go 132
      To Bring or Not to Bring?. 140
      T-Minus One-Day Anxiety 143
      Airport Day. 145
      Made It—Sort Of 148
      August 30th and Still Trying 153
      August 30th: Part II. 157

On the Road Again 158
An Aussie 164
A Minor Correction. 167
Week One 172
The Mesetas Begin. 178
Fingerprints. 182
Women 188
Contrast. 194
The Cruz 198
Two Days. 203
Twenty-Five Miles 207
Thirty-Six Hours 212
The Looking Glass 222

Epilogue–Part I. 235
Epilogue–Part II 247
Appendix One: Camino 101–A Pre-Walk
Camino de Santiago Planning Guide. 257
Appendix Two: Camino Related Websites. 261
Appendix Three: Questions for Discussion 263

Small Questions

They sat in my workshop. I'd seen them before. The faces are different each semester, each year, but the body language, questions, and facial contortions are about the same.

"You really walked five hundred miles?" The question came from the back before I could kick off the evening.

One spouse has brought the other to my session. Attendance for the second is reluctant, participation in the evening more an act of household harmony than of any real interest in the topic. One half of the couple wants to know more about the possibility and the adventure; the other thinks it a kind of semi-lunacy, with me as conductor. They seek only to get through the evening and return to the safety of home.

"And slept for a month in dormitory bunk beds with dozens of people sharing a single room?" the voice continued.

The questioner had an outwardly calm demeanor, the undercurrent an odd blend of genuine inquisitiveness mixed with a healthy dose of incredulity. I know the tone by heart, though I'm neither upset nor anxious about it.

At the beginning of workshops, I field questions of some similarity, in silence betting the attitude will change in the coming two hours. It's not that I'm that good a presenter. It's the subject matter. For reasons I can't fully explain, the workshop is compelling for those with even a little introspection and curiosity about the larger questions of life. I've seen this transformation overtake the great majority of attendees for the seven years I've been running courses.

Changing minds is not my objective as the evening starts, just the way it turns out by the time my last slide crosses the screen.

It was much the same thing originally for me too.

The Large Question

Ten years later, it all looks different. I had no idea when I started reading the pages that the day would alter my life. It was, after all, just another article, just another series from a fairly decent writer. But a decade down the road, it's been anything but the same old, same old.

In the fall of 2000, I stumbled across something far removed from my world. At the time, it didn't really spark my inner voice—the one that might have warned me—as it shouted "Hey! There's something more going on here." I didn't consider the newspaper series anything beyond a curiosity. Certainly it didn't seem like the kind of topic that might pull me into something larger. It was the novelty, the uniqueness that first caught my attention. The subject arose in a series written in my hometown newspaper. Thinking back now, there shouldn't have been even a passing interest. Not drawn to long, multi-page articles, I tend to skip such most of the time. This one ran over eight weeks, so it was even more likely to find the recycle bin early. Yet the newspaper series from the fall of 2000 pulled me in just enough with the first couple of paragraphs. Half a page later, I was fascinated. Several years later, I discovered many who eventually sat in my workshop sessions, were equally touched by that same newspaper series.

Two months of articles, one each Sunday, totaling some 25–30 full pages of the impossibly small type they insist on using. Despite my normal reticence, the Robert Sibley piece produced an anxious wait for seven subsequent Sundays. At the outset, I was not so much inspirited by Sibley's words as I was intrigued. By the third installment, for reasons I didn't understand, I was emotionally vested. Fascination grew weekly in a topic that had never before raised an eyebrow for me.

In the years that followed, my life seemed to be in an ever-so-subtle shift about this topic. One event seemed to lead to another, all building around this same theme initiated by Sibley. Over time, I eventually found myself looking through the years back to 2000, questioning whether something grander was at play in the events that had unfolded. The question eventually surfaced: Was there a guiding hand somehow involved in the cascade of events and circumstances?

It is the million-dollar question—one I was reluctant to ask too loudly in my earlier life. But with time and circumstance, the issue and the question gained weight. Was all this coincidence? Synchronicity? Or possibly some kind of divine intervention? It seemed there was something organized or perhaps orchestrated to the road I was traveling. The question has been chasing me since shortly after those autumn days at the beginning of the new millennium. My subsequent inquiry revolved around how to know, how to objectively evaluate the difference between these three.

Divine intervention is a big concept.

In the process of investigation, I seem to have ascribed the term on the front cover of this book as a more overarching theme suiting me: Fingerprints of God. I didn't know whether divine intervention and Fingerprints of God were the same thing. I'm not sure to this day I fully understand what the technical differences might be. The former, according to Wikipedia, is often described as a miracle. The Fingerprints term I now use as a kind of catch bucket for a range of things I attribute to God. Wikipedia hasn't got a page for this one yet.

My life has taken a number of turns over the last decade as regards this topic, and I've been exploring their cause and effect, wondering if God is in the mix that shifted the sands under my feet.

It's nothing new to have events take my life in a different direction. It's happened many times to me and lots of people I know. When such a change happens, I can't really say I give it much thought. Taking the changes in stride, I'm happy if the outcome is good and annoyed if not. When more events occur, seeming to support the first-directional change, so much the better—coincidence with complimentary timing. I was fine with this answer up until 2000, and even for a while after. What changed for me was the quantity and caliber of complimentary events that related to the Sibley series in the months and years that followed. There seemed to be a lot of them.

As they mounted in number, coincidence seemed to have a hard time standing up as the root cause. It appeared as though something larger—maybe synchronistic—was underway. With events seeming to follow a specific path, my questions grew and wouldn't go away.

Whether life involves some higher purpose, I've always felt a connectedness to something beyond myself. Any event sparking this inner connectedness is worthy of my mental energy. I think that was always the case, but I was rarely invested enough to follow a "trail of breadcrumbs." In the last decade though, I've developed a more introspective and curious attitude about such things. Maybe I'm just getting older. Whatever it is, the task of understanding coincidence, synchronicity, or divine inspiration as underlying influences in my world has moved more to the forefront. And that, I found, is where I lost my way for a while.

I have no more understanding than anyone else about how God works, and no specific insight or training other than the experiences of my own personal journey. I will admit there seems to be more spirituality revolving around my life lately. And like many, I suppose, it is comfortable to be on that adventure most days and not as much on others. Overall, it has been a fascinating journey, this developing spiritual side of my world.

My general thinking is somewhere out beyond synchronistic, events affect attitude and life in a grander way. But that as a general principle didn't get a lot of thought until a few years ago. Somehow, I now sense I'm gently but definitely altered, nudged in a different direction. It's subtle and hard at times to pinpoint or explain. And it is there, in some outer kind of place, where the investigation of cause and effect gets a little trickier. When events and their timing take on a more personal nature, my inner voice begins to call out and tell me synchronicity doesn't feel like the answer either. This sense of "personalization" is what drove my questions of something larger underlying the events changing my life.

I've been in sales with the high-tech industry for twenty-five years, working for companies like AT&T, Sun Microsystems, and the German conglomerate, Siemens. Professionally, my world involves the logical, the measurable, the scientific, and the accepted. Spirituality is a topic I kept to my private life for a long time and was reserved about discussing it openly. Until recently, I wasn't comfortable delving publicly into questions of faith. Lack of confidence, I suppose. I've felt others more qualified to tackle and debate such things—perhaps those more faithful or more studied. I don't feel qualified to tackle the concept of what some call "God incidents." It raises a few more million dollar questions, and I had less than a few answers. Still do. My only solution then, as now, was to follow the path of these things as they arrived on my doorstep.

So it was with the Robert Sibley newspaper articles over ten years ago. I understood the dictionary definition when his first installment appeared late in 2000; it created imagery of the ancient. It spoke to me of adventure, perhaps, of kings and knights, of fiction and history, of battles literal and spiritual. I hadn't really shifted my wandering impression when the articles ended. Yet any complacency I had starting the series was displaced, and I found myself pulled in, drawn toward action. I would long after refer to this unconscious transition as a sense of being "called." At the time, I didn't know the what or why of it, so I decided instead to simply walk into the world Sibley had painted. For whatever reason—instinct maybe, or perhaps it was that inner voice—something told me to be open to the unusual, to step up and give this thing a try.

Little did I appreciate the changes it would bring.

The promise I made after finishing the last article of the series was to literally follow the footsteps of the journalist at some point in my life. I decided late in 2000 to walk the eight hundred-kilometer, five hundred-mile Camino de Santiago, the ancient pilgrimage trail of the Apostle James, across northern Spain.

Though I didn't know it at the time, events would lead me to walk five hundred miles twice.

Out of the Closet

Sitting at the keyboard in an Internet café in Pamplona, Spain, it was not obvious what to write. I hadn't thought about what might be important to readers of such an unusual journey, what they might want to know about my pilgrimage. That I had committed to write about the adventure was even more a surprise, something I would have thought impossible as recently as a few weeks earlier. My trek of the Camino de Santiago was planned to be private, as I am inclined to be, especially about matters such as the long walk known widely as a pilgrimage. I had made no mental nor emotional preparation to answer questions about what I was doing or why. It wasn't for lack of effort—the problem was there weren't words to satisfy me, let alone something I could write for others who might want to know my rational. The purchase of a backpack and an airplane ticket to Spain had been completed without any greater appreciation of motivation other than just to go and walk the ancient trail. Crazy as it seemed, sitting in Pamplona, several thousand people now wanted to know how I was doing.

The e-mail letter, I felt, should offer a sense of my inner experience—it should be about the personal journey within. I arrived in Europe without expectations of the pilgrimage—a good approach according to websites I reviewed describing the trek. I suspect I was thinking of the trip more as a really long hike. Three days into my adventure, though, I was having difficulty understanding my feelings. Unexpectedly, I found more going on in head and heart than anticipated. A decent vocabulary didn't seem to provide words of adequate depth to describe the transition. Even had I been willing to share intimate details.

A heavy leaning toward privacy further prevented writing about this innermost change of attitude, something I now deem the real value of a Camino walk.

Instead, the keyboard pushed out a travel log—the names of towns visited, some basics of what had been seen, and the logistics and physical effort required for long hours of trekking under the weight of a fully loaded backpack. I dabbled for one brief paragraph about an experience of the unusual, maybe even spiritual. I wasn't sure. Writing about the great unknown and the unsure was not an easy place for me. I returned to the cover of descriptive scenery a few sentences after stepping beyond my emotional comfort zone.

It would be six years before I tried writing about it again.

The Sibley article, by then years behind me, explained an adventure of the Camino de Santiago as a simple path running across Spain. Traditional history of the trail holds it was a Roman trading route from more than two thousand years ago—a long dirt ribbon leading from Rome to Cape Finisterre, the westernmost spit of land in Europe. Until 1492 and Columbus, the cape was held to be near the edge of the world. Ships sailing west expected to fall off a flat planet. Oral tradition of the trade route leading across Europe claims the Apostle James navigated the path when he attempted to evangelize the people of Spain. Beheaded by Herod in a.d. 44 in Jerusalem some years later, James's body was returned to northwestern Spain by his companions. The Spanish tourist office today identifies the Emperor Charlemagne as first to cross the country to venerate the tomb of the apostle shortly after its discovery early in the ninth century. This and a similar journey by a local bishop seem to have sparked the notion of pilgrimage, traveling the route across the country to northwestern Spain, today home to the city of Santiago de Compostela. The cathedral in Santiago de Compostela houses the tomb in a crypt under the altar, and is said to still hold the remains of the apostle. The modern trail, commencing in St. Jean Pied de Port, France, at the base of the Pyrenees Mountains, follows across northern Spain, ending in Santiago de Compostela. The route is still, in this twenty-first century, thought of as a pilgrimage—a walk of the "Way of St. James," the Camino de Santiago.

History suggests the Middle Ages as the most populous time of the walk; stories support the journey of millions covering the distance during a seven hundred-year period. Given the lack of public transit, most walked from their homes in various other countries of Europe, eventually arriving in Santiago. Popularity waned in face of both Reformation and the Renaissance somewhere near the sixteenth century, with barely a trickle of pilgrims walking in the following five hundred years. In the mid-twentieth century, for reasons not entirely clear, interest in the pilgrimage walk resumed, and by the 1970s, the numbers were beginning to climb. In the 1980s Paul Coelho walked the Camino and shortly thereafter wrote about his journey as an allegorical story called *The Alchemist,* a book which would eventually sell many millions of copies. Notoriety grew further in the late '80s, when a visit by Pope John Paul II drew attention to Santiago de Compostela and the walk of St. James. Declaration of the trail to Santiago de Compostela as a world heritage site a few years before the turn of the millennium drew still greater attention, the population of walkers then growing to some twenty-five thousand annually. It was this increase in pilgrim walkers that sparked Sibley's attention. Why, he questioned, were so many willing to don backpacks, then sweat and struggle for a month to cover the distance from western France near the Pyrenees Mountains to Santiago de Compostela in northwestern Spain?

To answer the question, Sibley walked the Camino in the spring of 2000 and published his series—the same one I would stumble across—months later in the fall of the same year. The journalist arrived with only minimal preparation. Blisters, painful and bloody from trekking long distances without training, greeted the writer soon after he set out from France. Walking earlier in the year than commonly recommended, spring rains accompanied many days, leaving Sibley to arrive wet, tired, sore, and cold to the minimalist bunk house-style accommodations available each evening. At first read, it's difficult to understand how he might have inspired others to follow, especially me. The journey seemed a seriously unpleasant hardship.

It was the remainder of Sibley's writing, though, that touched something within. The journalist rested for a few days to recover his initial blisters, then pressed on across Spain, eventually walking the entire eight hundred- kilometer, five hundred-mile distance. He wrote of an extraordinary personal time—the quiet of walking forests, the majesty of traversing an entire country; of peace sitting alone in ancient churches; of extraordinary mountaintop vistas; and of winding, luscious wine valleys, and the austerity of arid plain. Centuries-old structures and towns dot the route, with some villages and cities dating back more than two thousand years. Crossing the sparse flatland of central Spain, he described as contemplative and introspective, reminding of forgotten memories of his long dead father. Sibley wrote of meeting other travelers from all over the world, fellow pilgrims as moved by their journey as was he, all willing to share life stories which, in any other setting, would be held back as intimate and private.

The experience moved the writer.

His description of the journey moved me.

My own father had passed away three years before the article was written. The loss was undoubtedly causing a shift in me—the result of which was that I spent more time considering what was truly important for my life. Perhaps it was this loss of a much loved parent, or perhaps something else caused the shifting. I had struggled through a divorce several years earlier. In 2000, I was a few years away from fifty, and larger questions of life's journey were increasingly occupying space in head and heart. Whether it was one of these milestones, some combination of them, or something else, I sensed a connection, a pull toward the long-distance walking experience described by the journalist. His story brought attractive images to mind—something of kings and knights and great works of fiction and the details of history. I don't recall the draw as spiritual or religious from that original reading in 2000; I wasn't aware of a connection with the concept of pilgrimage. Sibley had been clear about the Camino's reputation. It is a pilgrimage. At the time, I remember only the desire to attempt this strange journey and the sense of "needing" to do it. To explain this need to myself and eventually to others, I assigned the term *calling*.

Requiring a month to walk, plus travel time to and from Europe, I calculated the need for five weeks to tackle the Camino. A career in sales at a major computer company didn't lend itself easily to that much time off. So the Camino was not in my foreseeable future in late 2000. A consulting stint a few years later, and my new wife Sandra's layoff from her job freed us both to do the walk in that summer of 2003.

With still no greater appreciation of the word *pilgrimage* or a capacity to explain wanting to go, planning began for the five hundred-mile walk.

September 2nd of 2003 found me poking around the street corners of Pamplona, Spain, looking for an Internet café to tackle the e-mail letter I promised to write. Five weeks earlier, a casual lunch had altered plans for my Camino walk and dramatically shifted its context. That mid-July meal was what ultimately drove the need of an Internet café.

Seated at the Indian restaurant with me that summer day was Sandra and Father Joe, the pastor of a local church and, for some fifteen years, a good friend. I had updated Father Joe a few weeks earlier on our preparations to walk the Camino de Santiago trail across the north part of Spain. Sandra and I were planning to walk the Camino together. Father Joe had been pleased by the initiative but was unaware of the Camino until I mentioned it. Over lunch, as July threatened August, I came to appreciate that he had been inspired by the notion of pilgrimage.

The priest spoke of another parishioner, Caroline, who had recently shared plans with him of another unique undertaking. Caroline's fiftieth birthday present to herself would be a trip to an orphanage in Pattaya, Thailand, halfway around the world. There she intended to volunteer for more than two months in the fall of 2003. For the better part of ten weeks, Caroline would leave the comfort of home, family, and friends, choosing instead minimalist and emotionally challenging conditions, supporting some of the discarded youth of Southeast Asia. She had a plane ticket to Thailand departing September 22, some three weeks after the start of my Camino.

I knew Caroline but was unaware of her Asian plans until the lunch with Father Joe. Caroline hadn't known of our Camino travel, or at least she didn't until a few days after the infamous lunch. The pastor had an idea before we dined that day and, without hesitation, pushed his suggestion squarely into the middle of my private walk.

Father Joe explained a desire to encourage his congregation to place greater emphasis on charitable giving as part of their spiritual lives. Already a generous parish, my friend wanted to create focus for his parishioners, wanted charity to be a family affair, and have parents involve their children. His idea was to announce the travel plans, both Caroline's and ours, to his entire church at the Sunday services prior to our leaving the country for Spain. The premise was to explain the intended journeys and encourage the good people of his Blessed Sacrament Church to sponsor our walk, and the money raised would go to support the orphanage Caroline would visit. A few pennies per kilometer would be the suggestion. The church would collect pledged money and send it out to Thailand with Caroline to arrive in Pattaya with her.

Part of Father Joe's intention was to keep involvement in both initiatives as high as possible, which brought about a display map of Spain at the back of the church. It highlighted the Camino route for all to see. As my wife and I traveled, a pin would be moved along the route to show progress, the different towns and cities we succeeded in covering. I committed to write about the experience as we walked—my e-mail letter. Father Joe reciprocated with a commitment to post the e-mails on the church's website where parishioners could then read them.

The seed of my public letter writing was planted.

At the lunch in July, though, I was taken aback when I first heard my friend's proposal. On the one hand, the idea was a stroke of genius. The concept promoted good values and attitudes, called for action, fostered charitable giving, and encouraged great family behavior. It would raise money for a worthy cause and likely increase an already-strong sense of community among the parishioners. The price of Father Joe's inspiration, though, would be my privacy. It would be lost to the wind.

The prospect made me fearful.

I had been deliberately confidential about the Camino walk, telling almost no one of the intended journey beyond my immediate family and very close friends. Even among this group, I felt some questioned the undertaking. Sitting at lunch that summer day, a sense of real unease found its way into my stomach and halted my eating. I was nervous, the feeling a sense of personal exposure as several thousand people at the church would know of the planned walk—an eight hundred- kilometer pilgrimage—something for which I could not provide a motive.

The unease I felt was something I couldn't describe and didn't fully understand.

The other problem I felt was not voiced out loud, even to Sandra. It centered on our ability to actually succeed in walking the Camino, perhaps more accurately described as a fear of failure. The planning and preparation undertaken, I expected, would get us all the way to Santiago de Compostela, the destination city of the walk in Spain. But I understood I had no realistic idea of the effort required to walk five hundred miles. I questioned what might happen if it didn't work out. What if one of us fell, twisted an ankle, had some kind of health issue, or couldn't make the distance for some other reason? I had no measurement I could rely on to quantify the effort for this kind of an adventure. Worse, I thought back then, what if I was to have the misfortune occur shortly after starting out? What if I couldn't continue after only a small fraction of the distance? I was worried my journey might turn into some kind of public embarrassment. I had experienced a few of those from my school years decades before, and the negative baggage carried from those days had followed me through life. They had made me overly cautious about privacy. And none of this began to touch the idea of explaining why I wanted to walk a pilgrimage.

After a couple of days to think about the proposal, I calmed a bit, inner fear declining slowly. Caroline and Sandra had similar reactions. The three of us each determined separately that involving the church congregation was a good thing to do. Creating awareness of the needs of the orphanage and supporting a fund-raising event for such a worthy cause could not be allowed to flounder for our individual fear or an unwillingness to try. A couple of weeks later, I was cautiously onboard. Mild optimism about the revised approach arrived the weekend before we left for the Camino.

Four days before flying to Europe in late August of 2003, Caroline, Sandra, and I attended the services at Father Joe's church, me standing in the pulpit, explaining a walk of the Camino de Santiago. The pastor followed with an overview of the fund-raising, after which we all made ourselves available to the congregation, answering questions about respective plans.

By end of the day, I was overwhelmed by the response; support literally poured in.

Of great significance to my heart was the reaction of individual people to what had officially become my public walk. Hundreds came after services, each stopping long enough to offer words of inspiration, thanks, well wishes, prayers, and many, many kind thoughts. Others embraced us, offering unabashed kisses and hugs.

I felt humbled by their generosity and support and foolish for being nervous and reluctant a few weeks earlier.

On Monday, three days before departure, I bought a teddy bear to represent the people of the church. I christened it Pattii, a play on the letters but not the pronunciation of the city and orphanage in far off Pattaya, Thailand, where Caroline was headed. Unknown to me, Caroline would do the same, calling her bear Santiago.

Santiago traveled to Thailand on Caroline's backpack; Pattii would cross Spain strapped to mine. I went to Father Joe's church two days before our flight and collected a large white button used as a promotion item. The button reads 'the Spirit of Blessed Sacrament.' I pinned it to the chest of my little teddy bear. I wanted Pattii and his button to represent the people of the church, and remind me as I walked, of their generosity.

On the Tuesday morning, the parish secretary advised me the cash and pledges from the congregation totaled over $5,000. Some people called to say they were talking to their children to determine a family pledge and would commit to an amount within a few days. Still others called to voice support for the charity project and to say they were excited to be part of it. The total eventually climbed to $10,000.

I was greatly moved.

I was asked many times as I crossed Spain why the teddy bear with the large white button on its chest was riding in the middle of my backpack. On each occasion, I explained about the people of the church, their generosity, and how it had affected my walk, making it public. Each time such an exchange occurred, it seemed I or the other person was greatly touched by the kind act, and the connection of my walk to the Pattaya orphanage. Pattii was a beautiful reminder of all this as I walked, and of how my journey was profoundly changed as the result of a caring heart.

The two teddy bears came to be a lovely part of my walk of the Camino. Pattii was eventually sent to the orphanage in Pattaya, Thailand to share a display case with Caroline's bear, Santiago and hopefully be a reminder to the people there of the generosity of so many.

The events of that last weekend before leaving my home for Spain, intimidating as I had initially thought they might be, seemed to change something in me. In place of fear, I felt a close and personal bond with the people of the church. I was honored by what the walk had inspired and to be part of it. No longer was there worry about an inability to make the journey, nor did I feel any sense of being overwhelmed by the public event it had become. If we didn't make the total distance across Spain, so be it.

Curiously, I hadn't sought the change in circumstance that shifted my walk from private to public; it had come to me without solicitation. I wanted to resist being public. But the newfound purpose was enough that I swallowed nervousness, privacy, and historical baggage to stand for a few minutes and talk openly and publicly about doing a five hundred-mile pilgrimage walk. I didn't, on that occasion, try to explain the why of it. I spoke only of what I understood the journey to be, and of my intention to try to do it.

I committed to walk out loud for a reason greater than my desire for privacy. In doing so, I made a commitment to write of the Camino de Santiago journey, and again, without intending it, my voice became public on the subject of pilgrimage, at least on the one across Spain.

Without fully appreciating the transition, I had been gently drawn out of my fearful attitude and private world and became a face of pilgrimage for several thousand people. In some ways, the transition felt natural. In other ways, it was a strange twist on the road of my life. I still didn't fully understand the word *pilgrimage* as I prepared to set out in late summer of 2003. Nor had I yet begun to question the underlying cause and effect of increasingly connected events. This part of my transition finally occurred on our plane ride to Europe a few days later, that last week of August.

I found the question of divine intervention slipped into my consciousness, arriving without bringing the answer along.

The 2003 Walk

Five Letters, a Prophet, and a Shepherd

In western France, I stood outside the bunkhouse-styled refugio, taking in the moment, the morning air cool and invigorating. Still dark in the small French town, daybreak was not far off, the pitch black of night slowly giving way in eastern skies. Half an hour earlier, I had been in the rustic kitchen of the renovated horse stable, which doubled as overnight accommodation for pilgrim walkers, and put away a quick breakfast of fruit, yogurt, bread, and juice. Then it was back to the bathroom, hoping to encourage bladder and bowels to empty before venturing off to the wilderness of the Pyrenees Mountains. I was facing eight hours of crossing a high pass with no commercial establishments en route. Gathering personal belongings back at my bunk bed, I re-stuffed the backpack and declared myself as ready as I was going to be. I then left the confines of the refugio, the peculiar Camino-styled accommodation where I would spend a month revisiting the experience of this, my first night on a pilgrimage.

I didn't realize it standing in the silence of beautiful St. Jean Pied de Port, France, but the first hour of that day entailed what would become a ritual while walking. I would repeat the process in an almost identical manner every morning for the next thirty-one days. By the time I reached central Spain, twelve days distance from where I stood in France on August 31, I would refine the morning ritual of breakfast, bathroom, and re-packing to art form, never losing any possessions along the way.

"Let's go," Sandra whispered quietly through the blackness.

And with no greater ceremony, my wife started quietly down the cobblestones of the French village as I followed. The Camino registration office, where we had acquired pilgrim passports the night before—"credencials," the fellow behind the desk had called them—passed to our right. The heavy wooden door was closed, the place dark and silent. The first steps of the great journey carried me downhill, passed the centuries old row of stone buildings. I felt each had a history book worth of stories to tell. I imagined horses and knights riding the stone streets I now traveled. In minimal light, though, the street underfoot commanded my mental attention and focus. The gentle curve leads down and away through the arch of the Notre Dame gate of the ancient walled city, across the old stone pedestrian bridge, and leaves behind the historic district of St. Jean. I had entered the quaint little town barely fifteen hours earlier, was now headed out and away from the other side, toward something I still didn't fully understand, couldn't really appreciate.

It was surreal.

I was struck by the feeling of high adventure—a thought that, at the same time, was also a little scary.

My 2003 walk of the Camino de Santiago had begun.

The sages of the world are oft quoted as saying life must be lived one day at a time. And yet, for all the times we hear and read this, we rarely do. Or at least I don't. Time and again, I set a goal, a career path, or a personal objective—a destination for myself. On a regular basis, I measure how much I've achieved, how much closer I am to my goal; there is analysis and scrutiny at every opportunity. The question often raised is how to get there more efficiently, arrive a little sooner. Ultimately, much time is spent planning for and anticipating the future or worrying and regretting the unexploited opportunities of the past. Most often, it's both.

The resulting frustration is that I miss much of the present.

The Camino is an unchanging distance, ultimately unimaginable at the outset. Five hundred miles is comprehensible as a day's drive, an hour's flight, or maybe a long morning via a fast train. Time to cover the distance can be lessened by fewer stops in the car, an earlier flight, or maybe better train routing. Walking is a vastly different mode of transportation. Walking has little speed variation, usually with only one comfortable pace. Gentle.

The physical challenge of the Camino ultimately calls for great respect of the distance by those who set out. There can be no way of knowing whether it is possible to make it across the entire country. Most do; a few don't. Strength and endurance do not guarantee arrival in Santiago de Compostela. I met strong people who pushed themselves too hard and were lain up with shin splints, unable to walk farther without rest and recovery. And I would meet a man with Parkinson's who struggled to cover tiny distances each day and was prepared to walk for months, if necessary, simply to cover a third of 'The Way.'

He inspired me above almost all others.

Traveling on foot, five hundred miles is truly incomprehensible, not appreciated as that until a little time and a few miles have passed underneath hiking boots. Ultimately, I think it was my inner spirit that learned this first, learned to make the journey manageable and comfortable.

Physical capability is a large part of the equation, though a reasonably fit person can walk the distance comfortably. But I came to believe strength of spirit is a larger factor on the journey, learning to walk one day at a time the approach that enables the odd travel mode across Spain. By the time a few days have been spent on the path, it becomes evident the Camino is a long trek. The reality of the distance settles into the mind, then into the heart.

Facing west across the Iberian Peninsula less than sixty miles after starting out, I realized my destination was not so much hundreds more miles away, so much as it was weeks away. Distance became time early in my Camino. Somewhere near Pamplona, two days walk west of the French-Spanish border, the city of Santiago de Compostela seemed farther away than at the outset. Ahead, there lay two more mountain ranges, eight days of the open plains, and other aspects of the Camino still unrevealed. Distance measurement had shifted from miles and kilometers to days and weeks. I was already footsore at the end of each day, leg muscles well aware they had been put through more than my training program had prepared them to expect. Sandra had blisters on both feet and a backpack that no longer seemed well suited for her. There was no way to know when we might get to western Spain or even if we would. Less than half a week into the walk, I realized it was time to stop thinking about Santiago and its great cathedral.

I needed to simply walk each day and only that day.

And so the Camino taught me early on something I know well about life but rarely put into practice—that once headed in the right direction, to concentrate on what I need to do for the current day, to travel the best I'm able, and to enjoy the rest. The road of yesterday has been covered, good or bad. Tomorrow would arrive as it always has. My task, I realized, was to live fully in the present. This was to be life on the Camino—one day at a time. The mountains and arid, hot plains of tomorrow, the blisters, the aches, and whatever else was to come my way, these I would walk and worry about when they arrived. Whatever distance had been covered yesterday, whether all I had wanted or less, was behind. I would enjoy each day as I experienced it—the beautiful blue of sky, the green and black-grey of mountains close or distant, the scene of overloaded pilgrims strewn out along the dirt and gravel path, each simply putting one foot in front of the other. I was one of them.

I was a pilgrim. Or so I thought.

All this I took in each day as we continued to walk west.

I located an Internet café in the historic district of Pamplona, off a laneway where bulls run the streets during the annual ritual. There I spent an hour working the Spanish software to craft and send a letter to the good people of Blessed Sacrament Church at home. I wrote again on several other occasions as I traveled the country, in each of four other large cities conveniently one week apart, covering the month I spent walking across Spain. The letters here date from September 2003 and are based on the ones I wrote from the Internet cafés and sent home. They have been slightly edited to accommodate the context of events that followed my walk months and years later.

SEPTEMBER 2, 2003– THE FIRST LETTER

Well, our Camino walk has started, and so far, we've been blessed with perfect weather.

We arrived in St. Jean Pied de Port, France (SJPP), on schedule late Saturday afternoon. At the local Pilgrim's Office, we picked up our "credentials," a passport-like booklet identifying Sandra and me as Camino travelers. At the office, we received our first ink stamp in the credential to acknowledge our arrival. We will continue to receive stamps in the passport at all stops along the route. We also picked up a scallop shell each, a traditional icon of the walk. These are now tied to our backpacks.

SJPP is a beautiful, medieval-styled little place, a walled village set on a hillside with an old citadel guarding it from the top. At the edge of the historic district is the Notre Dame gate. It has part of a bell tower structure attached to a church of the same name. It is through this stone passageway that a traditional Camino starts. We walked through it on Sunday morning as the bell above tolled 7:30 a.m.

The street followed out of the old town, through the newer retail district and suburbs outside the ancient wall, until it led to farms and fields beyond the town. There we began the long climb up the side of the Pyrenees. Over the following eight hours, we wound along a narrow country lane and eventually onto a pathway that passed beautiful vistas and some of the most pristine and welcoming countryside I have ever seen. Throughout the climb, some 3,500 feet up over the 29-kilometer/17-mile distance, there were many flocks of sheep grazing the open fields. No fences held them in, and some wore bells to ward off the odd predator. The result was the sound of clanging everywhere across the hillsides, it somehow sounding a departure from conventional life.

Sunday afternoon, we arrived at the thirteenth century Augustine Monastery in Roncesvalles, the first town in Spain after crossing the Pyrenees. We walked across the border into Spain at a mountaintop pass a few hours earlier and then descended about 1,000 feet to our first overnight stop. Sunday evening, a mass was held in the stone chapel of the monastery, an event attended by all to receive a traditional blessing for the walk. Some 100 pilgrims gathered, most having walked over the Pyrenees. A few started their walk in Roncesvalles, the Pyrenees Mountain crossing avoided for health or other reasons. Accommodations in our first stop and apparently most others, are called refugios; in this case, one big room with over 50 bunk beds, his and hers showers in the basement. I'm learning line-ups and patience will be factors of the journey.

We added another 27 kilometers the second day of our walk and landed in Larrasoaña. The fellowship with the other walkers is growing as we share stories of blisters and sore muscles. The Spanish countryside is truly beautiful, as we are continually surrounded by mountains on this part of the trip. The path has been winding through the forests and fields of side hills and foothills, with the odd babbling brook alongside for further company.

An hour ago, we arrived in Pamplona, another medieval, walled city, this one made famous by the running of the bulls. It is a stunning city, with narrow streets winding between old buildings, every corner another magnificent church or cathedral. After I finish this update, we continue our travel west to a town called Cizur Menor, our destination for today. That makes another 20 kilometers, a total for three days of 76, almost 50 miles. We seem to have moved into a mode of focusing on the daily walking and not concerning ourselves with the overall distance. Meals, accommodations, and other necessities have worked out well without reservations and advance planning. We just walk and stop in any one of the many towns along the way. We could walk longer or shorter distances. The places we stop are simply the ones suited to the daily distance that works for us.

    We find our way along the trail following a very specific set of markers. The path is clearly identified with ubiquitous yellow splashes of paint posted here and there by "friends of the Camino." These yellow arrows are found on everything, from signposts to tree trunks, buildings, the roadway, bridges, rocks, and literally everything else that doesn't move. There might be the odd place where the arrows are not sufficient to find the way. But a virtual counselor on the Internet had suggested I should, at that point, ask directions of the locals or other pilgrims. As a minimum, it provides a reason to talk and interact with others. The approach has worked brilliantly.

    Pattii turned out to be a great traveler, adding little weight to my backpack. He has picked up a walking stick, a curious addition that came about in Paris, where we stopped for a day on our way to the Camino trailhead. We were having dinner when Sandra noticed a bucket of stir sticks for drinks on the counter, each stick a six-inch-long plastic item with tab on top. The tabs were all labeled "Saint James." We asked the bartender about them, to which the man displayed a bottle of Caribbean rum called Saint James. As further proof, he put an empty Saint James-labeled rum glass on the bar. It was an odd moment as Sandra and I sat at the bar with our just-emptied glasses, an unoccupied barstool next to us in front of the empty Saint James glass. With all the restaurants in Paris, I wondered about the odds of us sitting in this one, with the St. James paraphernalia. So Pattii now has a button on his chest identifying the Spirit of Blessed Sacrament, and stuffed under his arm is a stir stick I've christened the "walking staff of Saint James."

I have been asked by many fellow walkers to explain the Spirit of Blessed Sacrament button and Pattii. The story of your generosity is touching people from a lot of different countries.

I sat alone for only a few minutes after the second full day of my walk, dark of evening descending on the village of Larrasoaña, when he showed up again. Javier, he said his name was, Spanish for "Savior," it turned out. It was an appropriate name for the conversation about to unfold.

I had seen Javier earlier in the evening when initially I surveyed the tiny 10-block-long overnight town. He had been on the steps of the refugio bunkhouse earlier, barefoot, in ragged-appearing old clothes. Standing a few feet away in warm temperatures of the later evening, the man had washed dirt and perspiration away and was looking refreshed. Clothes, though different, still bore a well-worn look, clearly unique from the Lycra, nylon, and spandex of other Camino travelers. In another place, I might have judged him homeless. Despite older clothes, the man was clean and pleasant, with no discernable odor. On his feet, I noted a pair of sandals that had seen many, many miles. Javier had been barefoot earlier, and I wondered if he was walking the Camino barefoot. I couldn't imagine such a thing; it seemed a crazy way to walk such a distance. The smile warm and gentle, his face welcoming, the aura suggested a kind, well-developed soul within. Javier I estimated about thirty; hair and beard long, there was something of his overall appearance I couldn't quite pinpoint.

I don't recall his first words to me. I was more taken with his voice—unusually soft and calming.

After a few moments and several efforts by the heavily accented Javier to provide his name, the conversation paused, and he looked down at his feet. I asked where he was from, the usual first question posed to all pilgrim travelers.

Javier turned out to be Spanish—originally from the southern part of the country, I would learn in our conversation later. A self-described wanderer, the man had been walking much of Europe for the previous two years. He walked to Spain from somewhere in the north of France and was now traveling the Camino. Javier told me he often walked great distances barefoot, preferring it to sandals. He explained it to be easier to feel the earth, his words giving me the sense he treated the planet as a live being—another traveler, almost. The Spaniard described himself as a walker; he didn't own hiking boots.

I told my newfound friend of the apprehension I felt about walking the Camino—my worry that I couldn't explain my journey in Spain to the people at home. I shared my concern they might wonder about the sanity of my walking a 500-mile pilgrimage. Javier then told me the first of several things that would change the perspective of my journey, providing me different insight for my time in Spain.

"People think you are crazy for walking eight hundred kilometers in hiking boots. Is that different from those who think I am crazy for walking the same distance barefoot? Are we not simply choosing, you and I, to experience the journey differently? It is still eight hundred kilometers. People still think we are both crazy."

I had no answer for him. I was feeling sheepish for having earlier thought him odd for walking without shoes and then shallow for not seeing the obvious similarity he pointed out. His perspective made me realize the unintended criticism of my thoughts.

I then asked Javier the question I put to everyone I met.

"What do you expect to learn walking the Camino?"

His reply was immediate, his tone gentle, the soft voice remaining constant.

"I did not come to learn. I am here to feel."

The response was at once simple and overwhelmingly profound. I had a bit of a personal revelation at that moment.

I made a deliberate effort to minimize my hope of what the Camino might teach me before I left home for Europe. I had taken mental inventory to ensure I didn't carry expectations with me on the journey. I wanted to allow for any outcome, give every situation or conversation the chance to unfold in whatever manner it might. But I realized, sitting with the peculiar fellow in Larrasoaña, I was indeed expecting something. I was expecting to be taught by something called pilgrimage—a word I still didn't understand. I was looking for an intellectual outcome. Setting out, I had tried to open my mind to all possibilities so I would understand the new and the different during the time of my Camino walk. What I had not considered was something of an opposite. This journey offered heartfelt time, beauty beyond words, fascinating encounters with extraordinary people, and other ingredients of great personal experience. It is a place where my mind was free from multi-tasking, from the busyness of life. For the next month, I realized—as the words of Javier settled—my mind could take a backseat to all other senses. I came to appreciate this sitting on the bench with the unusual Spaniard. I needed to let my heart lead the way on this walk. I had to let my mind slow, even go to full idle for a while.

I needed to allow myself just to feel…

This simple thought would not leave me for the remainder of my time on the Camino. As I wrote these words years after my first walk in Spain, the concept had still not left me. But in that first moment, I came to realize another phrase had been in and out of my head for weeks before my first day at St. Jean Pied de Port. It had actually been with me since first reading about the Camino in Sibley's article three years earlier. I was coming to understand it had also been telling me how to travel the Camino. I hadn't fully accepted the message before my evening in Larrasoaña. The words I had heard over and over in my head rang out again:

Just walk…

I wasn't sure at that moment whether the thoughts were in my head or my heart. Sitting there in the dark of evening, I couldn't articulate any of them for the fellow sitting across the bench from me. Whether he sensed my lack of words or simply was comfortable in a one-sided conversation, Javier continued without much participation from me.

"My purpose in this world is to make myself better than I was yesterday," Javier went on.

"There is nothing more important I can do with my life," he said. "If I'm doing that, then I am fulfilling God's hope for me. I know when I am succeeding because I am not criticizing others or myself. I cannot make myself better by trying to bring someone down. If I make myself better, I will grow closer to God.

"Everybody is afraid in this world—this is why they are so often far from God's plan. We must learn to trust God. Walking is a way to overcome fear. It is a way to simply trust.

"When we walk, we see everything; we meet every person and experience what there is to experience. It is to get a better sense of God and his intentions. There is great beauty in all these things. When we drive or fly, we see nothing, meet no one, and experience little. We have no sense of God.

"As for the failings of others, anger, drugs, alcoholism, or anything else I believe is wrong, there is nothing I can do about these things. Only God can fix the brokenness of another person. But I can be an example for them through the actions of my heart. So many people feel they cannot make a difference in such a large world where so many things seem wrong. But one person makes all the difference. One heart can make everything change, make all things possible."

The words were profound, beautifully spoken, and penetrated deeply. Javier was describing a philosophy grounded in simplicity and spirituality—approaches I know well but practice in minimal ways. I find it easy to be critical, to judge others. As for trust in God, well, that's something I talk about but come up short more often than not.

Javier and I continued to talk for almost an hour in front of the refugio in Larrasoaña, the tone and topic much the same. Actually, it is more accurate to say Javier talked while I listened. As he did, I felt more and more touched by this unusual man, more at ease. He was clearly intelligent, wise well beyond his years. His faith allowed him to see God's beauty in all things, in all people. His trust in God allowed his heart to comprehend the simplistic yet profound nature of it.

As our conversation unfolded, I found my mind wandering to a time two thousand years earlier when James first walked this road. I wondered, while listening to Javier, what it might have been like to live in Spain when the apostle showed up. He would likely have worn old clothes like the man sitting with me, walked in sandals or was perhaps barefoot. He might have had long hair like my Spanish friend. James, I realized then, probably spoke gently and with similar wisdom. James spoke of God and of his love for all things. So did Javier.

My thoughts in Larrasoaña carried me to wonder how we—or rather I—so entranced by science, technology, and all else of the world, might discern a modern-day apostle or prophet. It was a great question to ask. I wondered, at that point, whether I had been talking to one for the last hour. It was in this thought I found the word I had been searching for earlier. Javier, I realized then, bore the appearance of an ancient prophet.

My philosopher friend said good-bye a few minutes later. The man preferred sleeping under the stars rather than indoors at the refugios. The Spaniard had apparently set up his sleeping bag underneath a bridge at a nearby stream. There he would be sheltered from the rain, if there was to be any this night.

I wanted to talk more with the unusual traveler. I left the evening's encounter hoping our walking pace during the days to come might cause our paths to intersect again. But further talks would not happen—the time in Larrasoaña the only occasion we spoke.

Curiously, that night, Javier had chatted only to me as far as I could determine. Other pilgrim travelers I met were sitting outside the refugio in Larrasoaña, positioned here and there nearby. For some reason, Javier had passed them by and sat with me. Later, when another traveler had come along to sit with us, the Spaniard had chosen to leave, saying nothing while the other person was with us. He spoke to no one else as he walked off down the street to find his under-bridge accommodations. Others would mention seeing Javier in refugios and along the path, commenting on his clothes, wondering if this strange fellow was crazy for walking in bare feet. I spoke to many people about him during the following weeks on the Camino. Many told me they had seen the wandering Spaniard and were curious about him, but none would tell me that they had spoken with Javier.

The experience left me wondering.

SEPTEMBER 11, 2003– THE SECOND LETTER

On Thursday afternoon, September 11, Sandra and I arrived with Pattii in the Spanish city of Burgos. This is one of the larger metropolitan areas we pass through on our journey, with a population probably around the 150,000 mark. I didn't see a sign coming into this city identifying its size, so I'm not sure if my population estimate is accurate. But it took over two hours to walk from the edge of Burgos, into the walled old town district in the middle. This had become my Camino way of sizing up a town or city.

Burgos is some 300 kilometers, 180 miles into our Camino walk. It is hard to believe we have already traveled such a distance and yet are only twelve days from where we started. Sandra has recurring blisters that are causing difficulties, but these are slowly becoming calloused. We both suffer sore muscles toward the end of each day. Backaches from carrying a too-heavy backpack are also common. But we continued to have an extraordinary journey. Pattii, our teddy bear, has a few scuffs from when I dropped my backpack the wrong way. Otherwise, he too is traveling well.

We start most every day at 6:00 a.m. The lights come on automatically in the refugio, and it's time to get up and get moving. The first order of business is to get out of bed quickly to get some bathroom space. The ratio of toilets to pilgrims—or peregrinos, as we are known in Spanish—was usually about 10:1. So you can appreciate an enthusiasm to get to the washroom with maximum haste and minimize waiting time. The next order of business is to get backpacks repacked. This can be an entertaining proposition.

The second night on the Camino, we shared a room with five people in it. That turned out to be the fewest number of people to sleep in a single room during our days on the Camino so far. The night before, our first night out, there were 110—yes, 110—people in one room. A big room to be sure, with fifty-five bunk beds arranged in rows and rows. However, most nights, we find ourselves sharing space with twenty to thirty people in one room. Usually two or three such rooms make up one refugio bunkhouse. I'm guessing this must sound a real hardship. But actually this is a part of life on the Camino, and after a couple of days, we got used to it. It works quite a bit better than one might imagine.

One of the major tasks to contend with out of this situation is getting organized in the morning. Given there are bunk beds in almost every refugio, the trick is to get backpacks repacked while several others are attempting to do the same thing, at the same time, all within a six foot radius of one another—side by side, as well as up and down. Interestingly, we have lost nothing (nor gained anything belonging to anyone else) in the first twelve days of this process. In some refugios space is such that two sets of bunk beds are pushed together, leaving one aisle serving four people. The first morning I experienced this, I expected a rush as some or all four tried to get to the floor first so as to claim the limited space and accommodate their desire to get packed and out the door. I was pleasantly surprised to find this was not the case. As I was swinging my feet out to the floor that first morning, the fellow on the top bunk on the other side was simultaneously doing the same. We both paused, and he then insisted I go first. He and the other three needing the single aisle waited quietly and patiently while I gathered my things and moved away to allow another access to the confined space. I noticed a similar interaction with the remaining three people after I cleared the way, and then realized the same thing happening elsewhere around the room. The other peregrinos are so pleasant and accommodating, this morning ritual, happens with surprising ease.

    I was curious to find I was so inspired by this small act of considerate behavior. I find more and more in my contemporary world that the sense of entitlement and the rush of daily life can often create a 'me-first' pushy attitude. Perhaps as I get old I'm getting more cranky, but there seems less civility in my world with the passage of time. In Spain, or at least on my Camino walk, that attitude was reversed. I was not only inspired by the gentleness of this small gesture, but it lifted me to behave better, more politely. And from this and other similar events there seemed to exist a kind of upward spiral among pilgrims. Virtually everyone exhibited this decent, kind and good natured style. Curiously, I found a warm, embracing feeling resulted for me from both witnessing this, and participating in it.

I was reminded how example encouraged a better me.

We're out the door by 7:00, with a quick banana and yogurt snack purchased at a local grocery store the night before. The morning walk starts in the dark, the later sunrise and shorter days a result of walking Spain in September and October. A later start means more walking in the afternoon sun, which brings the temperature into the mid 20s° C/70s°F on some parts of the Camino but a more uncomfortable low 30s°C/90s°F in other parts. By 7:30, we were seeing first light, and the sun is usually rising shortly after 8:00.

The first break of the day happens around 10:00 to 10:30. By then, it's time to find a local bar for café con leche (espresso with steamed milk) and a breakfast known as a boccadia, basically a sandwich served on a large, fresh baguette. The nighttime bars become the morning cafes—not much in the way of Starbucks in the country. Most days, we finish walking around 2:00 p.m. During the first third of our journey, we averaged twenty-five kilometers per day, about fifteen miles. There had been a couple of twenty-nine kilometers days, but they were exceptions. In the next few days, we start to pass through the central plains of Spain, and the distances are sometimes in the +30 kilometers / +18 miles per day range.

Our days conclude finding the local refugio for a stopover in the town of our destination. Getting checked in takes a few minutes as other peregrinos can be on a similar schedule. After check-in, we get to a bunk bed and head for a shower to wash off the sweat and dust of the day. Showers are as minimal as toilets so a similar situation arises as for the mornings. After showers, it is time to find a basin or sink to wash out sweaty clothes. The next issue is finding space on a line or railing somewhere to hang things to dry; we were always accommodated. With a few dozen others also washing clothes, it is surprising there is not more chaos.

But again, there is a rhythm to it all that works, basically because everyone cooperates.

The daylight hours are rounded out with a hunt for a restaurant and the dinner location for the evening. On that front, the food is anywhere between good and exceptionally good and is always plentiful. A grocery store for the next day's supplies completes the mandatory items for the day. Many people do some journaling to complete their later hours, and after time chatting with fellow peregrinos, it is lights out at 10:00 p.m.

The population of pilgrim walkers who travel at approximately the same daily pace as ours number somewhere between fifty and eighty. During the day, this group spreads out along the distance of the path to be walked that day, as some start out earlier or walk faster, some slower and later. There is usually about a dozen peregrinos in sight most of the time, although there are occasions when no one is around. During the first two weeks of our journey, we have become regular travelers with a few other English-speaking people: two women from Vancouver, a Scottish fellow, and a New Zealand woman. An American from San Francisco is also a regular traveler.

It is hard to put into words the feeling that comes about after walking such a distance day after day. Much of the lifestyle described above must sound like a hardship, yet it does not feel that way at all. The lack of space and minor inconveniences are part of a temporary lifestyle. We have heard virtually no complaining from anyone about it. But what is gained is a camaraderie that is very special. There is a shared sense of the journey, yet it is still quite personal for each individual peregrino out here. To a person, it is hard to describe.

I discovered I loved walking alone for long stretches every now and again on the Camino, Sandra at times ten to fifteen minutes ahead with other travelers. The silence and the stillness of the air around me I found exhilarating. By the end of my time in Spain, I concluded silence is one of the great pleasures, the true gifts of the Camino. It allows time for introspection, something that seems to run deeper and more intimate each passing day. There is a lot of chatter in the refugios every evening, pleasant as I was finding the quirky lifestyle there. But out along the trail, the experience is different. The path wanders through fields and forests, along streams and across open plains. It is away from traffic and road noise much of the time. It does travel in and out of a few large cities, but these are brief along the eight hundred kilometers of "the Way." When the journey does pass through populated areas, it is typically via small towns with little traffic moving about. Mostly, the path of the Camino de Santiago is away from the modern world.

Silence is truly peaceful for me.

The quiet provides me a personal space into which I found the outer surroundings produce an inner tranquility for my heart and soul. They seem naturally suited to each other, this inner peace and outer silence. The long days of walking offers a means to help the two reconnect. The quiet seems to create a naturally meditative state, which I love. Walking in silence, I can hear my heart, the voice within. It's a beautiful sound—clear, concise, and easy to comprehend what's going on inside when there is so little distraction outside. It seems there is so much to appreciate, all of it beautiful. Walking keeps my body busy, and my mind, with nothing to worry about, seems to drift into a state of proper rest and remain there. None of this was planned or intentional. It just seemed to occur. The Camino is a kind of natural environment for these elements to take the shape they do, or perhaps the better word is *reshape*. Knowing Sandra was nearby and safe was enough to allow me the personal time and space to float further into the world of pilgrimage.

Float indeed became the right term for how I experienced much of the time.

On one of these occasions when I walked alone, I came across a flock of sheep grazing a hillside. I realized as I drew near, no fence contained the herd. The sheep wandered freely across the glade, down an effervescent green rolling slope, and away from the path. Three dogs and a woolly bearded fellow stood watch over the herd at the top of the field, the man standing just a few meters off the edge of my Camino path.

It was a shepherd tending his flock; I'd never seen one before.

The scene was idyllic, given my inner state of peace. I paused briefly to take in the image, savor the moment.

Seeing me, the shepherd walked to where I had stopped on the path, coming to a halt only a few feet from where I stood. The dogs remained motionless as their master wandered away, the gaze of the three animals sweeping side to side across the hillside, eyes fixed on the roving sheep. The lone bearded man was tall; his clothes, that of a farmer, were well worn. A strap crossed diagonally over one of his shoulders, down the middle of his chest, connected to a cloth bag draped near his waist. His hair was thick, as was the beard, both dark but clean and neatly trimmed. A long walking staff in one hand completed the image. He was something of an old biblical figure. The man couldn't have better dressed the part had he been an actor in a movie.

"Buenos dias," came his call. It was matched by a hearty wave and a huge grin as the odd-looking fellow stopped a short distance from me. The ambiance emanating was cheery and good-natured. His eyes black, they almost danced with welcome, as if for a close friend.

I was barely able to respond before the man launched into a dissertation about something in his native tongue. I understood not a word of his Spanish as the shepherd continued on for a minute or so. From the great sweeping gestures, I assumed he was telling me what a lovely day it was. He was right; it was another perfect day in Spain.

"No comprende. No español," was all I could get in when I finally did interrupt. The Spaniard didn't break stride for a moment. Instead, my bearded friend continued his one-sided dialogue, not showing the slightest concern we didn't share a language. It took a few moments, but an unusual sense fell over me as he spoke further.

It didn't matter, I was coming to understand, whether I could comprehend him or not. This fellow wasn't in need of sharing words; he simply wanted to enjoy human contact. Communicating with words was the only available method. For we two strangers standing face-to-face in the middle of nowhere, I realized suddenly with great clarity, comprehension was optional to the conversation.

My heart ran back to memories of my father.

I flashed to the days during his last year in the nursing home. It had taken me a long time to understand how to interact with his Alzheimer's. My father and I had communicated easily back then, even though in his last month's words had not much purpose for either of us.

Language had begun to fail my father as the months of his disease turned into years. But our facial expressions and gestures, the smiles and sounds—these continued and eventually became far more important for me than any words that passed between us. The less my father spoke, the more I relied on pantomime, funny faces, and various contortions to interact, to get my messages across. As his disease progressed, the faces and movements I suspect became more bizarre to an observer who might look on, but remained effective, at least as far as I was concerned. Whatever I was doing, often thinking I probably looked ridiculous to anyone but my father and me, I found myself smiling broadly when our repertoire unfolded. My father had always smiled back, making his own funny faces in return. I'm not sure he knew me as his son during those latter times, and I came to accept it didn't matter. I am convinced he understood me as someone who loved him and offered his love in return.

It had been those outward, visible motions rather than dialogue that provided our ability to connect; our informal and silly sign language offered me such great pleasure back then. I came to accept our unusual communication because of its importance to me. I felt because I had had the right motivation and the right attitude, exchanging sentences was allowed to become optional for my father and me. Alzheimer's never defeated our connection. We were each with someone the other loved unconditionally. It was that personal bond of love that enabled our communication.

The shepherd had cared enough upon seeing me to take a similar approach and share a similar attitude. As soon as I understood that it was he who had it right, I followed his lead.

In English, I started to explain I was a pilgrim, a "peregrino." I had the presence of mind to get at least one word out of my mouth in Spanish. The other man nodded listening intently as I went on. The look on his face suggested he was hanging on to every word I spoke. In reality, it was the *sound* of every word he hung on to. I told the Spaniard where I was from and in his country for a few weeks to walk the Camino. He nodded again as he heard the word *Camino*. I told him I had left the city of Logroño earlier and was headed for the town of Nájera to stop for the night. The town names were familiar to the bearded fellow as well.

I felt myself grinning the whole time I talked—the same grin I had shown my father years earlier. It was immensely enjoyable, that few minutes the shepherd and I shared together on the sunny hillside. The Spaniard grinned back an equally child-like smile. I found it surprisingly easy to talk with the man, words being nothing beyond a formality. It was the sound of our voices we both heard; it was the smiles on each other's face we appreciated; it was the connection in our eyes that connected our hearts. We communicated easily, the Spanish shepherd and the Irish-Canadian pilgrim, both standing in a field at the edge of the dusty path for that few minutes in time.

It might have been a moment of grace.

In the end, I think he told me my destination was down the road about four kilometers. It might have been forty kilometers he said, but I hoped not. It mattered little. He waved good-bye and returned to his flock after a few minutes. I bid farewell to the gentle shepherd as I started down the path again, the all-too-brief friendship a memory I treasure to this day.

My smile lasted well into the next town.

My experiences of the Camino were often simplistic, yet the varied and unusual nature of them created a sense of the profound. Each event seemed to compliment the last, each taking me further into a more meditative inner place. As the days mounted, I softened, became more at peace with myself and the amazing journey I was on. Later I would refer to this transformation as the journey to becoming a pilgrim. I didn't notice it happening. It would be weeks before I even realized how much the walk changed my perspective. It was events such as my simple path-side encounter with the shepherd that changed something inside for me. Or rather it is more accurate to say it was the combination and timing of these events and curious meetings that affected me. The transition was gentle, subtle, and unconscious. I simply walked the path across Spain, and these things came to me as I journeyed.

I needed only to take them in, allow them to penetrate.

SEPTEMBER 18, 2003– THE THIRD LETTER

We are in a small town about twenty-five kilometers east of León, the largest city in northern Spain. We should be in León itself by sometime tomorrow. At that point, we will have covered approximately 475 kilometers—nearly 300 miles. Two days ago, on Tuesday morning, we passed a stone marker on the pathway identifying the halfway point of the Camino, 400 kilometers since our starting point. The journey continues.

Our updates home have been from the larger cities we pass through, Pamplona, Burgos, tomorrow León, Ponferrada in a week, and then Santiago de Compostela. These are the larger metropolitan areas with populations in the 100,000–200,000 range, León the exception with some 500,000. Their size makes them exceptions to other built-up areas along the Camino route. The majority of places where peregrinos stay are more the small town, tiny village variety, often with fewer than five hundred people. Most times the local industry is the family farm, with the refugio, corner store, and cafe rounding out a "commercial district." So we who travel the Camino are removed from the contemporary world in such places. Even when traveling in the larger cities, the refugios are always located in the historic or old town districts, usually a tenth-to-twelfth-century medieval-era sector in the centre of the cities. In Pamplona, this came complete with drawbridge and moat.

In the old town districts, cars and commercial enterprises are limited. All of this is to say the path—refugios and other aspects of the Camino—tends to make it quite easy to imagine a time many years ago, well before the modern age. The refugios themselves are often housed in buildings hundreds of years old. As pilgrims, we stay in monasteries, old farmhouses, grand old buildings, and even the converted stables of a lovely hacienda. Weathered stone walls, open-beamed ceilings, and cobblestone underfoot are common in many of these places. So although it is hard to imagine all the way back the two thousand years to the time of James, the lifestyle of medieval times can be very present in the daily walks and evening rest stops.

The Camino is well known in Europe and especially so in Spain. There is great respect for its history here and for those who travel its long, twisting route. So it came as no surprise that we have been exceptionally well treated on our journey. The people who run the refugios and the staff in the local restaurants, even in the grocery stores and pharmacies, welcome us with friendly faces and a "Buen Camino."

People along the Camino go to great lengths to accommodate a walker. Even more so it seems when the peregrino is from outside the country and cannot speak Spanish, as is the case for us.

The landscape changed considerably a few days ago. Burgos is a kind of dividing line between the rolling countryside, foothills, and Pyrenees Mountains, which lie toward eastern Spain and eventually the border with France. In the western part of the country, the scenery we expect to be similar. But in central Spain, to the west of Burgos, are the Mesetas. The Mesetas is to Spain what west Texas is to the US or the prairies are to Canada—quite flat, sparsely populated. Much of the time there are very few trees or other shade, and there is little civilization for long distances. We walk the Mesetas on our Camino trek as the trail continues westward from Burgos. It takes some eight to nine days walking to cover the central plain.

The food has been wonderful, as most restaurants have "peregrino menus." For around ten dollars we get salad or pasta, a meat and potatoes main course, dessert, bread, and a bottle of reasonably decent red wine. At one place they had run out of glasses, so our wine was served in beer mugs filled to the top. It put a whole new meaning to the phrase "having just one glass." There was considerably more laughter and merriment than usual in the refugio that evening. Moreover, the cost of walking is very low. Refugios cost about seven to eight dollars per night, breakfast a few dollars more. Thirty dollars a day does a good job of covering costs.

As Sandra and I were walking the Mesetas, we came to discuss how our priorities had changed to meet the demands of the Camino. Walking in the heat of the day as we do, water had become our first priority for most of the day, every day. We need between three to five liters each day, about a gallon, so we are constantly aware of our water supply and where the next fountain might be. We need food for all the walking we do, so it too is a high priority, but as fuel for the body and not for the luxury of dining. When walking in the hot sun, and especially across the Mesetas, shelter and shade are very high on the list of important things. And rest, though not sleep is also a top requirement. After walking for six to seven hours, it is amazing how much the body wants to simply stop moving and be still for an hour or so.

In our conversations, Sandra and I have also come to understand that other priorities have shifted as well. When I was on the plane traveling to Europe, the list of critical items included wallet, passport, and backpack.

As I took stock midway through our Camino, I realized that, though these things are still important, other items now are equally valuable to my journey and my heart. If somehow my backpack went missing, I would be in trouble without passport and wallet. But the thing I think I would miss more is my journals, in which I've written about this journey. My "credential," the Camino passports which I've had stamped at the refugios where we stay, reminds me of every stop I've made; it too is also on my priority list. And Pattii, with his "Spirit of Blessed Sacrament" button, and the "walking staff of St. James" are also on the list. Pattii has become more than a fixture on my backpack—so many people asked about him. His story and your generosity have moved many people, even those running refugios who see pilgrims by the thousands.

The teddy bear is now very personal to the journey and to me.

I located a stone wall along the southern edge of the tiny town of Santa Catalina de Samoza an hour later and sat motionless for a long while, admiring what remained of the open plateau of central Spain. For the first time in a great many days, I saw a setting sun. Everywhere I stopped along the Camino had been within the confines of a town, great or small. Whatever the size, narrow streets in every location meant the western horizon was blocked from view by surrounding buildings. Most evenings, unless I was inclined to walk to the western side of the town, the sun disappeared by late afternoon.

I don't remember making any effort to see a Spanish sunset until that day at the end of the Mesetas. In the twenty evenings that lay behind, feet sore from six to seven hours of walking each day, my body in need of rest, laundry, dinner, grocery, or drugstores and journaling, there always seemed activities to fill the late afternoons and evenings. Not that we were rushed. But between resting from the day's trek, getting food into our bellies, and preparing for the next day, time seemed to pass without much to spare. The pace was leisurely, but there were chores and activities to be done. Sandra would say in the months following our adventure she wished we averaged only twenty kilometers a day rather than doing the twenty-seven we did cover. The difference she felt would have given us more time to enjoy the evening stops.

I couldn't disagree with my wife's logic, but the pace we struck worked well for me. I liked the way the days and evenings passed. It felt to me the right balance of effort, activity, rest, and private time. There are reasons to average greater or lesser distances walking the Camino other than what we chose. My belief is as long as the available time doesn't force a pilgrim to travel too fast, as had been the case for a couple of women I met earlier, then it comes down to personal preference.

The pace of my Camino was opening my heart to feel the journey, as my Spanish friend Javier had suggested early on. I was experiencing something on this walk I don't often experience enough in my day-to-day life. In the simplicity of my days walking, I was unconsciously rebalancing my emotional and spiritual self. Feelings and intuitions normally pushed aside in the hurriedness of my daily world were allowed to breathe in Spain. There was air around them to blossom, to expose themselves more fully to my conscience. These, I am convinced, are connections to my heart and possibly to my soul. As the journey unfolded, I was moving into a space of still greater simplicity and inner stillness. Within these, I was beginning to hear the voice of God through the voice in my heart. The experience seemed to soften everything, allowed me to see greater beauty in nature, and feel higher emotion with the people I met. The blend of all these things created richness to seemingly every moment that lingered on long after the walk was over. There was a deliciousness to it I can't quite explain. I just knew I didn't want it to stop. It provoked the idea of walking forever, something I seemed to be entertaining more each passing day.

Maybe this is a taste of what heaven feels like.

Sandra and I both hope to walk the Camino again someday, both of us thinking we would do it alone next time. Walking together was the trip of a lifetime, something we shared and loved. Walking alone would be a different experience physically, emotionally, and spiritually. When that day comes, I suspect my wife will indeed travel more slowly. For my part, I will start out on the same pace and hopefully spend more time listening to my feelings about where to stop, whether sooner or later, as my heart might lead me to do. There are a few refugios and villages I want to stay in again. Otherwise, I would make an effort to spend my nights in different towns, at different refugios, and see the various parts of the Camino at different times of the day.

Resting on the stone wall at Santa Catalina de Samoza at the westernmost edge of the Mesetas, the mountains of León to be walked next day loomed large to my right. On the left, the last of the arid flatland flowed away from the slight elevation of the dusty little town and my sitting post. I realized the scene before me was the last I would see of the central plain that had seemed so intimidating only seven days earlier.

Curiously, I felt a strange sadness that I was leaving the Mesetas.

I think when I started to cross the central plain I thought the great open space presented an obstacle in the way of my progress, my journey. I had positioned it as a challenge to be conquered, defeated somehow by effort, by strength, by force of will if necessary. I had unconsciously defined the stark and beautiful land an adversary.

It was a very human approach to something I didn't understand.

A week later, sitting on its far edge, crossing the Mesetas felt nothing like a win. Nor did the land seem in anyway defeated by my crossing of it. Rather I felt more as though a partnership, perhaps a friendship of sorts, had somehow formed between us, the great open plain and this pilgrim traveler. We had somehow come to respect one another in the days we had been together, with me discovering the austere beauty of the barren Mesetas, the land now seeming to whisper an acknowledgement of my willingness to feel the journey.

I had come to connect with the spirit of the Mesetas.

This austere character of Spain's flat central plain had removed even more external distractions for me. Towns are farther apart, leaving more time between where there is only open country. The sky seems endless. The predominantly flat land is at times devoid of trees and scrub, akin to the mid western plains of the US. It was there the experience of solitude took me deeper within, to something I felt was a greater access to my soul. The first two weeks of the Camino can be about getting accustomed to the physical, of walking six, seven or eight hours each day. After almost fourteen days, entering the Mesetas, the physical was behind, and the central plain allowed a more introspective time where solitude brought inner understanding and still greater clarity.

When it was done, I felt, in a way, as though I didn't want to leave, wasn't ready to move on. I questioned, as I sat, if it was the Mesetas itself I would miss. Or perhaps the feeling was also about the parting landmass being a major milestone of my cross-country walk. I was coming to realize that slowly but surely I was covering the great, previously unimaginable distance of the Camino. I was beginning to appreciate that one kilometer after another, I was indeed moving across its eight hundred-kilometer length and toward its end. Santiago de Compostela was drawing closer. Almost six hundred kilometers lay behind me to the east, 350 miles. Less than a third of the Camino remained ahead.

I was coming to sense, as the journey continued, that I was not entirely happy about the prospect of my walk ending. The trek across Spain had initially seemed endless, an almost impossible task to accomplish when first I set foot to the eastern side of the Pyrenees Mountains some three weeks earlier. I hadn't understood pilgrimage then. I was still coming to a full realization of it crossing the Mesetas. With the time and miles that lay behind, pilgrimage was indeed penetrating me. It wasn't something that I understood so much as it was something I felt. I was appreciating pilgrimage as a pure experience of body, heart, and soul. It is a way of being. There is an indescribable beauty to it to which words cannot do justice. As I sat on the old stone wall, well past the halfway point of my Camino, I came to understand this. I came to appreciate it as the passing days were carrying me deeper into the world of pilgrimage. And yet there was also an uneasy feeling accompanying this change that less time lay ahead than had already passed underfoot.

I didn't want the feeling to end.

The beautiful moments of sunset in Santa Catalina de Samoza brought emotion I wasn't expecting.

The twinge of sadness within surprised me.

Sandra took a picture of me just then as I sat on the wall in Santa Catalina de Samoza. I was unaware she had returned and was standing only a short distance away. The camera lens pointed south, our overnight town behind my wife and out of sight of the viewfinder. On the right side of the picture she took, the first few hundred vertical feet of the next day's mountain trek is visible. I'm sitting midframe, staring south and east, nylon and polyester the hallmarks of a modern pilgrim. A near-crumbling stone wall supporting me, the last of the Mesetas is just out beyond where I sit, the burnt and brown soil of the flatlands mixing with soft green—telltale signs of the coming hills and departing plain.

That shot is one of my favorite pictures from our long trip. The time on the wall became very emotional for me. That afternoon and evening felt like the last hours spent with a friend who had somehow become very close in a short time. We traveled the distance together, the Mesetas and I. It had become a spiritual encounter. As I sat watching the last of the day's light cast ever-longer shadows, silence reminded me the time had come for us to part.

The Mesetas had become almost another peregrino to me—one that I didn't want to leave behind.

I sat until the sun disappeared.

I felt a bit like Javier, the ancient prophet-like fellow from my second night on the walk. He had spoken with great reverence about God's creations, all of them. I was reminded of his attitude sitting in Santa Catalina de Samoza as I felt somewhat as he described. Reverence was what I felt for the land I had just crossed. The Mesetas had taken on great purpose as I journeyed across the country. They reminded me my travels are not always as pretty or as easy as I would like, yet there is great beauty in everything, even the starkness of austerity. I simply need to be willing to see it. My time in central Spain brought this home and touched my heart in a way I had not expected. I never thought of myself as appreciating emptiness. But the Mesetas I discovered were not empty; there was simply a greater absence of distractions.

It was my attitude that changed during my days there.

SEPTEMBER 23, 2003–
THE FOURTH LETTER

Time is now flying by.

We are in Ponferrada, west of the Mesetas, and in between two mountain ranges. Over the last two days, we climbed the mountains of León and then descended about two thousand vertical feet down the backside, covering some thirty kilometers, eighteen miles, both days. At the top of the last mountain we crossed is the Cruz de Ferro, a wooden pole with a cross on the top of it. Around the base of it is a very large stone pile, accumulated over many, many years. This is the place where peregrinos place a small rock they have carried here from their homes to place with the rocks everyone else has left over the years. The tradition dates back even before the time of the Apostle James when the Celts made pilgrimages to Cape Finisterre. We left a stone we had collected from our home and also placed a small scallop shell on the pile given to us by a parishioner at Blessed Sacrament Church.

The day after tomorrow brings another mountain range and another two thousand or so feet up and down. But for the next few hours, all is flat. Not long ago, we crossed the six hundred kilometer mark; there is now less than two hundred kilometers to Santiago. One hundred twenty miles. It's hard to believe how much distance we have covered. I find I want the time to slow down.

I have noticed a couple of paradoxes about the Camino.

James, what little I know of him, evangelized in Spain for several years after the apostles dispersed. For all his time here, his efforts produced only a few disciples—less than a dozen in all. Not much success by any measurement that might be applied today. But to travel through Spain, or at least the northern part of it as we have, is to acknowledge the extraordinary ripple effect of his work. Spain is one of the most religious places I have been.

Every town, even the tiny ones where we have stayed so often on our Camino journey, has a church, usually quite a beautiful one. They stand in the middle of the towns, often on a hill where they can be seen from a distance. All churches have towers with bells. In the larger cities, the cathedrals are magnificent. Surprisingly, even when there are great cathedrals, there are also many other churches close by. The bells ring in many of them, so we have been greeted or bid farewell in many towns by the sound of a bell tolling. It has been lovely and felt quite personal to this journey. It started with our first steps as we walked through the Notre Dame gate and out of the old town of St. Jean Pied de Port more than six hundred kilometers ago. The bells tolled then and many more times since.

The other paradox of this journey is how few spiritual conversations I've had. I was expecting, given the nature of this journey, it might be foremost in many discussions. But I came across a poem the other week that described how difficult it is to put into words why many people are here. Even trying to understand the questions is not necessarily obvious.

I have met many people whose stories have touched me, some deeply. I'd like to share a few with you.

I mentioned Javier earlier, the young Spaniard who spends as much time walking as he can. He could easily be passed by as a homeless person but had a gentleness and peace about him that spoke volumes. He said he was here not to learn but to feel, to grow and better himself, and, by doing so, to be more connected with God. He said he knew he was doing these things when he was not criticizing others.

I walked for a week or so with Kinsey, a fifty-year-old from San Francisco. He is here as a birthday present to himself. When he started going to church again in the last few years, he realized that he had never read the Bible. His companion for his eight hundred kilometers is an ultra-light, portable CD player with an audio copy of the Bible on it. He figures he should have time to hear most of it.

Jann and Elishia are a fifty-something couple from Maastricht in the Netherlands I met briefly last week at one of the refugios. They told me, as have many other Europeans, that a pilgrimage should be started from home. Last year, they walked the first 500 kilometers of a 2,300-kilometre, 1,400-mile walk from Maastricht to Santiago. Then in May of this year, they resumed their journey from where they had left off last year. They will arrive in Santiago late October.

Bill, sixty-five, I came across in a small café in the town square of Carron de Condes, a settlement on the Mesetas. He is from Canada and was planning to walk the Camino in 2004 but changed his mind and is doing it now, as he discovered next year he might not be alive to walk.

Almost everyone I meet says they are here as a response to some kind of a call, some sense they should walk the Camino. For many, perhaps me as well, the "answer" why may not become apparent until months or years after leaving Spain. But all seem to feel the same need—to just walk.

One of my favorite stories of people I met is about a lone fellow we came across a day's walk after Leon. My assessment of the old man was that he was possibly dehydrated, maybe even sick. This was the second opinion of the man I had formed within the previous twenty minutes, and it would also turn out incorrect. My first impression had been that the man was drunk. Arm in arm, we escorted our fellow traveler the extra block back to the café and resumed seating positions where packs and coffee had been left minutes earlier.

Away from the torturous heat, the fellow introduced himself. As he did, he stood at the end of our table, fumbling with his backpack, trying to get an upper-chest buckle undone. After a moment, realizing he could not succeed, I offered to help, continuing the unbuckling ceremony to lift the weight from the man's shoulders. I realized, as the bag fell away, Trevor, as he had identified himself, didn't have strength or the flexibility to get his pack off without great difficulty. Even with assistance, the mundane task seemed an ordeal.

We offered coffee; our guest requested a coke. Sandra and I sat together on one side of the table, the unusual peregrino across from us on the other. Trevor told us he had come to the Camino from Britain. Sitting with him at the table, his words were more intelligible than they had been half an hour earlier when I'd first encountered the Brit at the edge of town; perhaps it was more that I was, by the time we sat together in the café, listening properly to his voice.

The gentle old man went on to explain he suffered advanced Parkinson's disease. My inside started churning immediately; my eyes filled with water as I began to fully comprehend the man's physical challenges.

Trevor hadn't been stumbling, as I'd assumed when I'd first seen him cross the road earlier on the edge of town. Nor had he been staggering as he worked his way down the sidewalk toward the refugio and our café. By the definition of our healthy bodies, Trevor didn't walk at all. What he did was more a shuffle. I had often seen older people move in such a manner. In my father's case, it was just before he was restricted to a wheelchair at the nursing home. I had seen Pope John Paul II move the same way as the old pontiff crossed the upper room of the papal residence a few years earlier when a chance meeting had brought Sandra and me there. It was the stricken movements of a body infirmed with age and a crippling ailment.

The air in the café became at once so thick I felt I could barely breathe. A great sense of shame filled me, so dismissive had I been toward this gentle soul. I couldn't believe after spending three weeks on the Camino, walking over five hundred kilometers on what was a spiritual pilgrimage, that I could still be so quick to judge. How easily I had misunderstood the old man. How absolutely and stunningly wrong I had been about him.

As we talked more, the Englishman provided insight to the extraordinary struggle he endured each day. I calculated our daily distance and compared it to Trevor's.

Sandra and I had left the outer edge of León that morning. Given the flat terrain, we traveled at a pace of five kilometers, or three miles per hour. It had taken us the morning to cover the twenty-five kilometers from Leon to the village of St. Martin where we sat with our coffee. Trevor explained he had left León on Monday, five full days earlier. Like us, Trevor set out early each day, walking about five hours before stopping. But while Sandra and I might walk six or seven hours, Trevor was exhausted and unable to continue after five. More significantly, his pace was barely five kilometers *per day*. The old Englishman was walking the Camino at barely one kilometer per hour.

Trevor's plan was to walk to Santiago from León. As we sat at the table, I knew the distance to still be some 300 kilometers, 180 miles. Trevor had over 90 percent still to go. The Englishman would be walking Spain for the next two months at least, assuming he made the distance at all. The old man claimed he had no fixed time to return to his homeland. Trevor intended to walk until Christmas, some four months away, if that was what it would take. He was determined to walk to Santiago de Compostela. I felt certain he meant it. What I couldn't appreciate was how he would actually succeed.

I found myself wondering how Trevor managed his Camino logistics.

The old Englishman walked alone. I didn't know his age, and given the Parkinson's, it was hard to guess; he looked every bit of late sixties, maybe seventy. How did he deal with his pack? He had been literally unable to take it off a few minutes earlier in the café. What did he do about everyday activities, the tiny refugio bathrooms, cold showers, bunk beds? And where did Trevor find the time and energy to search each local town and village for his evening dinner and daily supplies? Did he need medicine for his journey? Was his health at risk if he couldn't get medication out of his pack? How did he carry enough water to last the many hours between towns? Often the distance was five kilometers—a day's walking for the old man. What did he do when the distance was ten? Where was his family, and how could they allow him to be here alone?

I felt at that moment as though God tapped me on the shoulder. It seemed, to me at least, God's way of telling me that coming across the old man with Parkinson's was anything but coincidence or chance. The meeting instead felt very personal. I felt a great connection to God in those moments sitting with Trevor, though I couldn't explain why. I reflected on the chance meeting often over the weeks that followed the few short minutes in the bar at St. Martin. I eventually came to see the episode with the Englishman as helping me understand a truer meaning of what it was to see everyone, to feel deeply no matter whom I come across, no matter what they look like. It was the same lesson presented by my meeting with Javier. Everyone deserves proper dignity. It took a time, but I eventually came to sense there had been extraordinary purpose in the meeting with the Englishman.

I would come to feel, as I continued to walk the great two thousand-year-old path, that very few of the people I encountered were coincidental meetings. Instead, I came to see my time and these connections as a place—an intersection in time, if you will—where God could deliver messages more easily to me. I sense there was no greater reason than because I was more open to them. My heart was open. I listened for my inner voice. I paid attention to conscience and intuition. I left the Iberian Peninsula feeling I had a better understanding of how God speaks to me. Most of the time, my life is dialed into a high-speed zone, and God's messages go unheard and unheeded. There were encounters I experienced on the Camino I'm inclined to call mystical or at least leaning in that direction. Some events were small, some profound.

Some, Trevor and Javier among them, I could only call deeply moving, spiritual in every sense.

The encounters and the quiet time that followed gave me a chance to reflect on such events. Reflection offered a sense my life is being guided or can be if I'm paying attention and willing to trust what's happening. I assessed the experience as related to belief, maybe faith—giving God enough room in which to operate. On the Camino, it seemed I was doing a better job of this than I had in the past.

I wondered what changes I needed to make to let more of this guidance into my everyday world. Yellow arrows were guiding me along the path. It struck me that figurative yellow arrows, maybe spiritual in nature, also existed out there somewhere in my daily life.

It was something of these I felt I experienced along my walk of Spain.

OCTOBER 1, 2003–
THE FIFTH LETTER

We made it; we have arrived in Santiago.

On Tuesday evening, about 6:30 p.m., September 30, we walked into Obradorio Square in the heart of the historic district of Santiago de Compostela to be greeted by the spectacular facade of the Cathedral of St. James. The flight of stairs into the church was the last remaining steps to be taken. The square was full of people, many of whom we had met and walked with from time to time over the four weeks and three days since we started out through the Notre Dame gate of St. Jean Pied de Port, France, on August 31. It was quite an emotional moment.

Several days earlier, we stopped for the night in a small town called Triacastela. Triacastela is on the west side of the Sierra Mountains, the last significant terrain to be traversed on the way to Santiago. From there, it was about 130 kilometers, 85 miles, of rolling countryside still to go.

It was there the peregrinos, me included, began to talk for the first time since leaving France, of when we would arrive at our destination. Until then, we had all taken the approach of walking the distance of the particular day: twenty, twenty-five, thirty kilometers and the local town for the end of the day. Santiago was always a great distance away, too far to be thought of in detail. But by Triacastela, the most strenuous walking was behind. Blisters had healed, and calluses had replaced them. Occasional aches and muscle pains had become part of the journey and came to be accepted. So barring some sort of accidental injury, the distance that remained was something we could all expect to complete. There was a festive feeling to that evening. But it was a bit premature, as the 130 kilometers still proved to be as challenging as any other part of the Camino.

We had at that time been traveling with a sixty-year-old fellow by the name of Gert from Denmark. A lovely and gentle person, Gert had just retired from his career as a university music professor. He had described for us the "Tree of Jesse," a solid marble column inside the front entrance of the Cathedral of Santiago one morning on our walk. It was there he explained he expected to be deeply moved at the end of his walk.

A days walk after Triacastela, and still several from Santiago de Compostela, Sandra and I stopped on a cool morning to rest and rejuvenate with a large steaming café con leche. The Celtic cottage-like refugio we found had emptied of the previous night's pilgrims. Though many of the refugios close during the main hours of the day, the Celtic cottage remains open to serve passing walkers. The place was silent when we entered, save for a couple of thirty-something women who operate the overnight stop. The main dining room within was something of a scene from a novel, with a dramatic and steeply-sloped ceiling of heavy wooden beams supporting the exterior roof. A huge stone fireplace, thankfully with a few lit logs, covered one corner. Matching stone walls and well worn floors spoke of a century's old building which had seen many world travelers come through its doors. Entering the room that morning was like being wrapped in a warm blanket. A few minutes after settling in, Gert came through the front entrance, and joined our table near the crackling fire. It was there the topic of the marble column in Santiago came up.

Gert began to explain the tradition for arriving pilgrims completing their walk.

The Camino is traditionally concluded in the entry way of the Cathedral of St. James in the city of Santiago de Compostela, now less than fifty miles away. In the entrance of the church is a stone archway, known as the Portico of Glory. The center of the arch is supported by the marble column Gert was referring to. Some fifteen or so feet in height, a statue of St. James is affixed to the front of the column, towards the top. An intricate carving of the Tree of Jesse, a Biblical image relating to the family lineage of Jesus, adorns the front side of the column just below the statue. A short distance below that, and still a few feet from the ground, there is the impression of a hand; four fingers and a thumb. The impression has been worn into the column as arriving pilgrims from almost 1,000 years place their hand on the column as a gesture of thanksgiving for a safe journey. The tradition has created an indentation in the marble—the fingers and thumb of a right hand, the marks left by literally millions of pilgrims who followed the tradition for over a millennium. Gert had tears in his eyes as he imagined putting his own hand into the impressions where so many had done so before him, and thereby add his own journey to the history of the column, and the pilgrimage. It was a deeply emotional moment for Gert in simply explaining the upcoming arrival, and his tears caused mine and Sandra's to flow. I realized when he spoke, that in a short time I would do as Gert described, and I too would become part of the history of the Camino.

The thought was powerful beyond words.

The cathedral is not restored but is a magnificent structure with twin spires stretching some twenty stories skyward, a separate bell tower in between the two completing the upper facade. A grand stone staircase marks the entrance from the cobblestone square below. Just inside the main front door we found the column Gert described, about two feet in diameter and fifteen to twenty feet tall, with the statue of St. James on top. The biblical Tree of Jesse is carved on the front. We had hoped for quiet time to reflect on the moment, but the cathedral is a major tourist stop, and large crowds filled the church. The moment had to be shared with many others, not all with the experience of having walked a great distance to get there.

I was reminded at the moment when we arrived at the cathedral, that it was not the destination I came for but the journey. It had been a spectacular one, long and difficult and at times painful to be sure. But it had been a journey filled with countless beautiful moments, images I will never forget; meetings with other peregrinos, some of whom became very close in a short period of time; the hosts in the refugios; proprietors in shops and stores; a shepherd here, a prophet there. The walk was a time of slowing down sufficiently to see every face I passed, to get a proper look at every field and mountain and stream. It was an opportunity for great personal reflection.

Once in Santiago, we received a final stamp for our credentials and a certificate confirming our journey and its completion at the cathedral. We attended the noon mass for the pilgrims the next day where the celebrant read out a list identifying how many had arrived the previous day, their starting point, and nationality. It was a special moment when he announced two Canadians had arrived in Santiago from St. Jean Pied de Port.

Over the last day and a half, I have run into many people I met while walking. Some had traveled with me recently; some had not been seen since the very early days. I was met by all with a huge hug and a kiss on both cheeks. Each was a wonderful reunion, and congratulations had a special meaning, knowing these others had a personal understanding of what the journey had entailed. The square and surrounding streets were often filled with the same scene over and over.

The original intent is to stay in Spain until October 10, but somehow, with the remaining days, being a tourist does not fit in with what we experienced in the last month. Without understanding the how or why or it, I have become a pilgrim. So an earlier flight will be likely, although plans have not yet been made. This trip will be only about the Camino, and on another occasion, hopefully we will return and see more of Spain.

Early that last Friday morning in Santiago de Compostela, a few days after completing our walk, I left Sandra at our hotel and crossed town to pick up our rental car. Up before sunrise and wanting some air, I went out to cover the ten-minute walk to the Parador Hotel with the Hertz rental office two hours ahead of schedule. The office would not open until 9:00, but I wanted to retrace the streets of the historic district one last time before leaving.

Santiago, I realized in the quiet of dawn, was like the rest of northern Spain: late to bed and late to rise. Wandering the nearly deserted streets of the city alone on that last morning, the quiet was almost eerie during what to my normal life should have been rush hour. I strolled passed the cathedral, thinking to take one last opportunity to visit. I stuck my head in the side door of the eight hundred-year-old church to find a wonderful surprise. The building was virtually empty; the vast inner space was dimmed and silent save for a single set of footsteps echoing a slow pace around the perimeter ambulatory.

Cutting across the nave, I located a pew close to the front and drank in the beautiful embrace of absolute quiet. I felt a peace in the great building for the first time since arriving in the city. The cathedral had been busy and noisy on my arrival in Santiago. Coming in from the peacefulness of my walk to a cacophony of camera crazy tourists, I returned to the church several times since my initial, frustrating visit. Each time since had been a variation of the first visit; Santiago has become a major sightseeing locale, the cathedral and its artifacts central among places for photo opportunities. Each day I entered for mass, for a private visit, or to seek other pilgrims, I encountered chaos, the same disturbingly loud voices, the same disrespectful use of video recorders and cameras. Each occasion I left feeling disappointed, experiencing no more spiritual connection than the day I arrived.

In the silence of the great building, I started to lose myself in thought early that last Friday in Spain, the quiet of the majestic space comforting; my sense I was now a part of its great pilgrim history.

I had become a pilgrim myself.

The quiet, though, did not remain so for long. A middle-aged couple arrived to seat themselves two rows behind a few minutes later, the pair arguing in another language about something I cared not a whit for. With what had to be fifty rows to choose from, I was annoyed they had felt the need to come within earshot of me. I turned to offer the couple a most ungrateful look, the male half of the couple looking up momentarily and then returning unfettered to the agitated conversation.

I rose disappointed and headed for the door.

I couldn't win, I decided. I had finally found a time when the church was empty and tourists not disturbing my peace. It was at that exact moment the couple in the throes of domestic dispute had dropped in and upset my private time. I let out a sigh of displeasure as I passed what I considered to be interlopers. They appeared not to notice.

Along the ambulatory en route to the backdoor, I came across something I hadn't acknowledged on previous visits. A side chapel, not unlike a small, elegant cave, sat just through an opening along the northern wall of the cathedral, part way toward the rear of the building. Double glass doors partitioned the area off from the main hall, the word *silence* emblazoned across them in great large letters and seven different languages. Clearly I wasn't the only one suffering the persistent noise problem.

Pulling on the glass, I entered, discovering no one inside. I found the front pew again, this time with only a half dozen rows to choose from. Again, I dropped into the seat. Silence fell around me one more time. The door behind opened less than a minute later.

I felt I was about to lose it and almost offered a loud complaint to the latest intruder.

Thankfully I didn't.

A tall man strode slowly up the centre aisle of the quiet little chapel immediately after I entered. The fingers of his left hand wrapped tightly around the stem of a chalice; his right hand on top steadied the square envelope and covering cloth, the chalice material identically colored to the man's garments. The priest was fully robed to celebrate the 8:00 a.m. service at the Cathedral of Compostela with but one participant.

Me.

I stood to acknowledge the priest and his intention, knowing the process of mass from both practice and a little booklet I brought with me explaining the service in English. By the time the biblical readings started, three others had joined our little congregation, the Spanish padre oblivious as to whether any of us understood his language. The priest offered communion bread to those present when a bell, high above in the tower outside—the one between the giant spires of the cathedral—let out a single peel. I felt my heart jump, my mind retracing steps across the previous five weeks. It settled on Paris and my first day in Europe.

I remembered a single bell toll at a church near the Eiffel Tower, a place I had stopped to say a quick prayer the day before we caught the train south toward the Camino trailhead. The bell had rung once—one bell, one toll. Sandra had been outside, resting in a nearby square, and had not heard it. I remember thinking it odd at the time, the peel of the bell coming from within the nearly pitch-black of the darkened building. I had seen no one else inside, yet the bell sounded from within, not from a tower. There was no reason I could appreciate for its sounding; it was not due to the hour of the day nor for any ceremony commencing or completing. It seemed to have been rung by an unseen hand. I remember at the time feeling odd, as though the bell rang for me—a sense I couldn't in that moment explain.

The next time I heard a bell there was again just a single strike; it occurred as I walked through the town gate in St. Jean Pied de Port when Sandra and I took our first steps along the Camino route. I had heard another bell, one peel again, in the little town where we took cover under the side porch of a church in the heavy rains during the first week of the walk. It had happened on several other occasions before then, but by the time it rang at the church in the rain, it seemed too often to call coincidence. I heard single bell tolls in many of the small villages and towns along the Camino—always one bell, always one peel. I did acknowledge they occurred most often as I arrived or departed the villages along the Camino route. I continued to hear them as I traveled the entire distance of the country. On one occasion, while walking the open flat plain of the Mesetas, I remember coming into a dusty little town and thinking as I passed the local church I hadn't heard a bell for a while.

The steeple peeled once at that exact moment.

My eyes had watered.

As I sat in the little side chapel of St. James Cathedral in Santiago, I couldn't think of an occasion when there had been more than a single strike of the bell in all the times I heard it. I hadn't been counting, but it happened on something like a couple dozen occasions between Paris and Santiago. The single bell toll during the church service on my final morning in the city of pilgrims caused my eyes to water again. This time, as I knelt immediately after communion at the Friday morning mass, my Camino walk concluded. I had come to acknowledge the bells as a spiritual communication of a sort, telling me I had been accompanied as I followed the path across Spain, to just walk and allow myself to feel the experience of the Camino, to become a pilgrim. I had done that. The bells I had come to accept helped me understand I wasn't walking alone.

The bell in Santiago would be the last, although I didn't know it as I knelt in the little chapel of the sacred old building. I didn't hear another bell during the rest of our time in Spain, despite visiting many other churches in the five days remaining before our flight home. I rose from the pew a moment later, instinct for some reason calling me to leave a few minutes before the mass formally ended. I pushed out the glass doors, the main hall of St. James Cathedral outside the chapel very much empty. The quarrelling twosome of earlier had disappeared; the huge church once again bathed in silence.

I was overflowing with rich emotion.

Though empty and silent, I felt the great space issued no sense of aloneness. A very spiritual presence had taken me, powerful but gentle, the feeling warm and embracing within the ancient building. I walked quietly to the back of the church in that moment, understanding with great clarity what to do.

I located the great stone archway separating the nave from the rear of the church and looked up at the carving above the doorway—the Portico of Glory. I was finally alone in the vestibule near the main doors of the building, no noise or tourists to disturb my moment. The stone artwork seemed vastly more beautiful in the silence of that particular morning. In the privacy of the moment, a special kind of peace penetrated me. I seemed to feel the scene above me rather than see it.

I let my eyes follow down the carved Portico figures, along the line of the marble column supporting the arch from below—first over the statue of James near the top, then on down the remainder of the pillar. Intricate carvings followed the entire length. I knew from the explanation of others I was gazing at a representation of the Tree of Jesse.

According to the Bible, the Tree of Jesse follows the blood lineage of Jesus through the Old Testament from the beginnings of spiritual history. Somehow, that history felt for me a part of my final morning in Santiago, a reminder of it beautifully set into the front side of the marble column holding up the Portico of Glory. Five fingers, a hand imprint, were visible a few feet off the floor just below the bottom carving of Christ's family tree. The impression had been worn into the column by millions of pilgrims from a thousand years, each placing a hand against the marble in a moment of silent thanksgiving for a safe arrival. I had been unable to experience that personal moment when I arrived in Santiago three days earlier—the crowds posing for photos at the back of the church had blocked my path.

I felt I understood my Camino pilgrimage with a new sense of wisdom as I stood at the back of the cathedral on that last morning. I had come to feel the great journey in my heart and appreciate my purpose for being there was to just walk, to follow the path and offer simple trust, meeting people who would touch and inspire me. The profound experiences of the Camino had found me. Or perhaps it is more accurate to say they had been placed in my path. I uncovered them by simply following the ancient dirt trail, allowing the experiences to unfold around me, rather than pushing away to adhere to schedules and expectations. I had finally come to have real inner trust; accepting my needs would be looked after if I was willing to simply follow my heart and be open enough to give credence to my inner voice. These are lessons of life for me, simplistic but difficult to practice daily, learned anew on the Camino with heartfelt purpose and true wonder. I would never forget the feelings and experiences of my long walk and of my last minutes in the cathedral of northwestern Spain. It had become an amazing spiritual journey touched by the presence of God. I understood in my heart the true meaning of pilgrimage.

Unknowingly, I had become a pilgrim.

The church was still perfectly silent. I slowly positioned my hand over the grooved impressions in the pillar, one by one slipping my fingers into the marks created by millions of other travelers from the past millennium. Tears poured instantly and uncontrollably down my face. The moment was so intensely emotional, so spiritually personal, I barely understood what was happening. I stood motionless, engrossed; the purest and most intimate feelings I can ever remember flowed within me. There was a sense in that moment of great clarity; it seemed obvious and without question for me.

I knew where had I come from, who my greater family is.

I would remember later that I finally appreciated what Gert, my Danish friend, had tried to explain a few days before my walk concluded. The retired music professor-come-pilgrim I met almost a week earlier, the two of us forming a deep bond in the last few days we shared walking together into Santiago. In the Celtic cottage, over coffee that one morning, Gert had described the impression in the marble column. With profound passion, he had explained the moment of arrival when he would place his hand where so many others had, joining himself to the 1,200 year history of millions of Camino walkers. His effort to describe the event had brought tears to the older man's eyes.

During the emotional and personal moment in the vestibule of the church, my hand in the centuries old marble impression, I felt intensely connected with the Tree of Jesse, to the family of God. I couldn't remember such a feeling before. I felt as well a deep, personal connection with another family—that of pilgrim travelers, present and from ages past. The connection I felt as I stood alone in the great hall under the Portico of Glory was unquestionably of God, powerful beyond my capacity to explain it. It was one of the most beautiful experiences I could ever recall.

I slowly removed my hand from the column near the back of the Cathedral de Santiago a minute later, wanting to ensure it was I who released the moment and not have it interrupted by the arrival of others.

Hands by my sides, I stood facing the pillar for another long minute, saying a proper good-bye to my Camino. I turned then and quietly retreated toward the door. I remembered as I pushed through the exit, feelings of a similar moment from a few days earlier. It had been at the edge of the forest when I walked the last kilometers to Santiago de Compostela where I heard a jet engine running up to take off speed at the nearby airport. Sandra and I had spent the last day of our Camino walking some twenty miles to the outskirts of the city where we would conclude our trek across Spain. As we neared the city limits, we exited the last forested portion of the pilgrims' trail. It was then I had turned to look back at the trees as we walked out into a clearing near the airport, and left the greenery behind. I had a feeling that somehow the Camino was bidding farewell to me just then; it seemed a parting of souls, at least for a time.

I had had a similar feeling in Santa Carolina de Samoza my last evening of the Mesetas.

As I headed out the doorway of the Cathedral de Santiago early on the Friday morning three days after walking out of the forest, I looked back one last time at the stone carvings and the interior space near the back wall of the great church. The forest had been, I sensed, a farewell to my physical Camino, the walk itself; the morning alone in the cathedral had been my thank you to God for traveling with me on the journey. His response, I felt, came in the rich emotion of an extraordinarily personal moment at the pillar with the handprint.

A combination of sadness, joy, and tranquility mixed in my heart as I left the church.

The sadness relatively light but undeniably present, I knew with certainty my Camino walk had come to a close. I didn't want it to end. The joy I felt permeated my entire being. The Camino experience had been richer, fuller, and more beautiful than anything I could have imagined. The overwhelming feeling however, was of tranquility. A deep and profound peace settled on me as I exited the sacred building for the last time. I had found an intimate, personal, and spiritual conclusion for my walk of the 1,200-year-old pilgrimage.

The clouds hung heavily grey in the skies over Santiago when I moved into the chilled morning air just before 9:00 on the Friday morning. I stood for one last long look down from the entrance platform just outside the doors of the church, gazing across the Plaza de Obradoiro square to the hotel on the far side. I descended the stone stairs a few moments later and crossed the cobblestones to the Parador hotel a hundred meters away. Completing the paperwork for a rental car a short while later, I drove the circle route around the perimeter of the old town district, picked up Sandra at the hotel where we had been staying, and drove away from Santiago de Compostela.

Sandra and Me on Our 2003 Walk

Climbing the Pyrenees Out of Western France

Ad Hoc Group of International Pilgrims

Early Morning on the Camino

Walking the Sierra Mountains

Camino Marker Along a Forest Trail

Trail Markers at Sunrise

Typical Camino Traffic on a Village Main Street

Pilgrims Tailgate Party

1100 Year Old Pilgrim's Bridge at Hopital de Orbigo

River Crossing Built By Friends of the Camino

Refugio at Santa Catalina de Somoza

Refugio at Boadilla del Camino – The Mesetas

Typical Refugio Bunk Room

Journaling at the Estella Refugio

Town of Molinaseca

Cathedral of Leon

Contemplation at the end of the Mesetas

Arriving at Santiago de Compostela

My Compostela – Certificate of Completion

Patti, his Walking Staff and The Church Button

Sandra and I spent the last few days in Spain working our way toward Madrid for a Tuesday flight home. Our return had been scheduled for a week later, but we had come to understand how much we missed home and family. Over a glass of wine somewhere in Santiago de Compostela during our time there, I realized we were not sightseers, not tourists. I had become a pilgrim on this peculiar journey. Sandra too. Pilgrimage I had come to appreciate, was a feeling, a set of beautiful and powerful experiences, large moments measured by an individual heart and shared with other hearts that were also undergoing transformation. The experience of pilgrimage, and its transformative nature, is not well captured by words found in a book, this one or any other I have read. It is a deeply personal experience, one touched gently and beautifully by the divine.

For me it is about a firsthand experience of God.

Basking in a small square in Santiago de Compostela on our last day there, watching the interactions of other peregrinos there developed an appreciation, an understanding of this; and I realized I wanted to end my journey of the Camino in pilgrim mode. Tuesday had been the first available flight out, leaving us several days to get to Madrid. Avil, Salamanca, and Toledo consumed the available time to cover the distance, each a place of great spiritual and historical significance. We spent many hours in the magnificent squares and plazas of each; sipping wine, snacking tapas, and simply letting the peacefulness of the pilgrimage and our remaining time permeate.

A giant cobblestone plaza, Plaza Mayor, in central Madrid became our last. It seemed to find us at the perfect hour that final day. Bordered by grand old stone structures, the wondrous architecture of the country was something I still found entrancing after nearly six weeks of savoring it constantly. We sat for the late afternoon hours, simply admiring the beauty of the day and our surroundings. Street musicians played soft, classical music to accompany our emotions and time in the plaza. Wine and tapas soothed our spirits further.

I was deeply saddened when the sun finally dropped behind the western wall of Plaza Mayor in downtown Madrid on the Monday evening of October 6, 2003.

My adventure in Spain had found its closing time. Though I missed home and family immensely, I had come to love the country Sandra and I spent almost forty days exploring. The time had been slow, lingering and lovely, natural treasures and breathtaking history playing a part of the walk. But it was unquestionably the amazing inner journey of the Camino that had brought about deep, deep feelings of the heart. I had been touched as never before. How much of it was the people of the country, how much of it was brought on by the other walkers, and how much was about God reaching into my heart to touch my soul, I will never be able to say. I have lovely memories of all.

It is a rich, rich memory, one that will last a lifetime.

I returned home to rediscover the overwhelming beauty of the people—many hundreds and perhaps thousands—who supported our journey with prayers, well wishes, and personal gestures. The greetings and kindnesses we received our first weekend back touched me greatly. It was only then I came to appreciate one of the greatest aspects of my pilgrimage. I had initially wanted my Camino walk to be a private event. Standing among the crowd that first Sunday back from Spain, sharing stories with many who welcomed us home, I finally understood how much less the journey would have been had I gotten my wish.

I had a bit of a personal revelation in that moment.

As the last weeks of 2003 brought the year toward close, my pilgrimage of the Camino was under intellectual review—how it had been inspired, how it became public, and how the unusual events led to an unexpected experience of my humanness and my spiritual journey. The question of coincidence, synchronicity, and divine intervention returned.

I came to accept, as I reflected on the journey of my pilgrimage, there had been much divine intervention. I didn't seek it out. I was gently introduced to the concept of pilgrimage—something I hadn't and couldn't imagine before the newspaper articles of 2000. Turns in the path of my life were not always apparent as my attitude shifted slowly, the decision of which way to go not obvious until faced with a choice, a fork in the road, as it were. As the decisions arose, the options of which way to turn remained open—my choice—while the direction always seemed clear. Once taken, the new direction felt natural, even though I found myself occasionally in situations that weren't at first easy. There was trepidation, even fear on a few occasions, such as when my pilgrimage moved from private to public. I expect there may be more of this as the path ahead reveals itself. But any occasion of unease was dispelled quickly and replaced with an inner calm. The outcomes have been universally welcome, for me, for Sandra, and for those beyond me affected by the journey—the physical and the spiritual one. For me, this is perhaps what most distinguishes God from coincidence and synchronicity.

I have come to think of these turns in the path of my life as a kind of spiritual equivalent of the yellow arrows I found painted along the dirt trail running across northern Spain. Both the life turns and the yellow arrows have taken me places I've never been, wouldn't have gone without something to point the way. Both have produced beautiful, heartfelt experiences I would not trade for anything. I have a new sense of spiritual arrows—ones that seem to offer a means for me to navigate; though following the signs, I have found, requires a level of trust that I'm still working on. Following a path without knowing its destination or outcome is at odds with my contemporary way of thinking. I've come to understand this as a characteristic of the spiritual journey, but I need to accept it more within my heart. I rarely know the path ahead; sometimes even the next few steps seem obscure. Yet if I simply persist, continuing one step at a time, the next arrow appears when I need it.

Trust is building over time.

More than anything, there is a feeling of great and peaceful humanness rising out of the experience of pilgrimage. Day-to-day life seems more vibrant, the presence of God more apparent. I'm developing a comfort in the way both interact; daily human life, and this sense of God's direction within it. They suggest paths I might not take, might not otherwise even see. I hope they represent growth as the direction of my journey unfolds. I find the ways of God offer a special gentleness and loving style.

My task is to give a bit of room within for all this to move about.

The Second Camino

The Path Back to Spain

As the plane lifted off from Madrid airport a few days after leaving Santiago de Compostela in October of 2003, I promised myself I would return, walk again. Many times during that first walk I wondered how the journey might feel different were I to travel the distance alone. Sandra and I spoke of it often as we trekked, questioned whether an opportunity might present itself for a second adventure across Spain and how each of us wanted to try it solo. The experience Sandra and I shared wanted for nothing. Yet I felt something called me to plan on going again by myself.

At the time I expected, other than for this hopeful promise, pilgrimage and the Camino would soon become afterthoughts, a memory like so many other trips I've taken; details fading to a blur shortly after getting back to my work-a-day world.

It was not to happen.

I was asked repeatedly after returning home by people who had contributed to the walk fund-raiser for pictures of my Camino journey. Each occasion I affirmed I would bring them along sometime, feeling it the least I could do for the generosity that brought $10,000.00 to Pattaya and the Thai orphanage. As requests grew in number, there seemed more than a passing interest in the trip. It also seemed many were inquiring of the inner experience more so than the images—what had it felt like, what did I gain from the journey, and was it spiritual. Part of me was excited to share the story, and part of me nervous and not sure how to do it. I'd had no experience speaking publicly of such subjects; I was still reserved about sharing the spiritual, the personal, and the intimate. I finally got over my nervousness, when I was approached a few weeks later by a small group of people at the church. They proposed the hall of the building as an ideal location to put on a slide show. There the many contributors to the $10,000.00 orphanage donation could see the Camino pictures and hear my description of twenty-first century pilgrimage. I was out of excuses to avoid a public talk and though I was still a bit reserved before the event, as the evening approached I started to actually look forward to it.

A couple of hundred people watched my slide presentation for two hours one cold evening early in 2004, most staying after with questions more personal than I had readied myself to tackle. I found an unexpected sense of ease with the unusual and intimate of the topic and thoroughly enjoyed the conversations that lingered long past the planned time. One in the audience suggested an idea that would keep pilgrimage and the Camino alive for me long after the beginning of that year. Leslie, a friend of my wife, attended the presentation and was fascinated by the interest my audience showed in the curious topic. Continuing education courses at the local high schools is a sideline business for Leslie, and she questioned whether there might be interest beyond just the one group who had shown up at the church. She hoped I might be the fuel to offer another series of classes for her business; she saw me as workshop leader. I agreed to let her try a promotion for one class, thinking it wouldn't amount to anything.

Six classes filled to capacity within weeks, each one after the first encouraging Leslie to request my availability for another time slot and another session. Fascinated by the interest, I seemed to push aside my reservation about getting deeper into the topic. I did worry the only presentation I had done had been shared with a relatively known quantity—people I knew by name or by church association. The continuing education classes would bring unfamiliar audiences with more questions and a more diverse set of beliefs and opinions. I didn't feel ready as I launched into the first workshop a short time afterward.

Two thousand ten brings my seventh year of workshops. Many classes later, the initiative continues, with my passion for sharing the Camino continuing with it. Any discomfort has long settled, and I've learned to simply offer answers as best I can, whether about logistics, the deeply spiritual, or anything in between. Curiously, my interest in a second walk was kept alive by these continuous presentations of my first walk. Of the many who've attended my workshops, several hundred have since traveled the Camino. I usually receive an e-mail before their actual journey, some with an extra question or two, others simply telling me I had inspired them to give Spain a try.

They inspire me.

It's the return e-mails I treasure. Trepidation about the effort to walk five hundred miles accompanies almost everyone before their journey. This and the general logistics weigh heavily before the trip: how hard is it; what about carrying a backpack; is there an issue dealing with the language; how about the weather—does it rain; how hard is it crossing the mountains and what's it like sleeping in the refugio bunkhouses—these are the most common and perplexing issues. Universally, travelers return awed, almost all claiming their walk the adventure of a lifetime.

As 2009 opened, I found myself unemployed courtesy of the economic fallout from the subprime meltdown. My sister's husband, Michael, a man for whom I feel great love and affection, succumbed to cancer in June of the same year. Sandra's mother was also taken by cancer in the closing months of 2008. It was a time of losing great people too early. With work and the economy slow to resume, I found myself with time to consider another walk. I had hoped my second walk would fall in 2010, but realizing the economy was starting to show signs of life, work opportunities I assumed would as well. By mid-August of 2009 I had made the decision to return to Spain, the beginning of September again the target for setting foot to the trail.

With the topic of pilgrimage and the Camino still in motion in my heart, I determined the repeat journey would include a public blog about the experience. I was dumbfounded at the time to explain how this came about—it just happened. With a determination to step fully away from my shyness, I committed to write publicly about the spiritual and emotional journey of pilgrimage as I experienced it. Writings from my first trek had barely touched the intimate side of the walk. For the 2009 sojourn, I wanted to offer a full description the inner journey my Camino might bring about.

This is my blog.

FOUR DAYS TO GO

Last time planning was six months ahead of the curve, the decision made in spring of 2003 to head for Spain during September of that year. Lots of research, planning, details, and the like. This year's Camino sojourn was committed to stone a little over a week ago, around August 15. My ticket was booked the following day, and I've been training like a mad fiend ever since.

Late the 28th of August, less than a week from now, I'm off to Frankfurt with a connection on to Madrid. I should have checked the corresponding train and bus schedules needed to get me the rest of the way to Roncesvalles or St. Jean Pied de Port (SJPP), one of my two possible starting locales. St. Jean Pied de Port is the French town on the eastern face of the Pyrenees, where I started last time, the traditional kick-off point for many walkers. Roncesvalles, the first village in Spain, is notable for its position on the western side of the Pyrenees, taking the mountain trek out of the equation. Given my late decision to do the Camino and limited (read not yet adequate) training, I'm not sure which place to head for.

The airplane ride is a points flight, and I got it with almost no notice, something akin to winning a lottery. I booked right away without the rest of the travel details covered. My connections to the Camino trailhead take me north from Madrid into Pamplona, probably via rail, then hopefully eastward by bus for either of my two destinations. Trouble is the Madrid-Pamplona train arrives at 6:30 p.m. daily, and the last eastbound bus leaves a few minutes earlier. So I don't have an elegant plan yet for getting out of Pamplona, which leaves me some fifty or eighty kilometers short of the respective starting towns. My hope is to start walking August 30th; the reality may be the 31st.

With luck and no broken or seriously damaged body parts, I should arrive in Santiago de Compostela the last day of September, leaving one to two days to put my feet up, sip a little wine in the cafes, and relax. My fondest memories of Santiago is reconnecting with walkers I had met somewhere during my month long walk. Those were occasions of great emotion—strangers only weeks earlier, the people I met had become immense in my heart. Such a chance encounter on the streets of Santiago was to instantly fall into a huge hug, a smile of loving satisfaction, and the understanding that we were somehow joined, perhaps eternally, as fellow pilgrims. I cherished those last days. They were immeasurably beautiful. I hope for the same in slightly more than a month.

Last time, I created a conditioning program that started three months before launching off to Spain and my walk across country. This 2009 walk has two weeks of prep supporting it. I fear my body is not going to be happy...

My brother-in-law, Michael—Mikie—once told me my body would protest more each year after fifty with aches and pains, especially in my joints. I blew through fifty without a whimper, but by the time fifty-two arrived, I had to admit Michael was right. I now hear creaking within and worry about bits falling off. Seriously, though, my body needs more time to recover from anything strenuous and delicate handling to kick start each day. I'm not decrepit, but the years have become present in my bones.

I walk train four hours a day, have been for eleven days now, and will get in a few more sessions before Friday's plane ride. I'm getting up at 5:00 a.m. to build them into my day. Each walk covers about fifteen to eighteen kilometers, or nine to eleven miles. I feel good, there are no bleeding parts, and endurance is building reasonably well. I've logged about 160 kilometers / 100 miles in the last ten days. Problem is the first ten days in Spain will see me cover almost twice that distance and include significant mountains and foothills. I'll also be shouldering an eleven-kilo/twenty-five-pound backpack with whatever worldly possessions I think I need to survive a month in deepest, darkest Spain.

I'm not sure I'm physically ready. I'm worried about shin splints or another ailment forcing a layup by the time I've walked the several days back to Pamplona. It's not that sitting still concerns me or any pain that might accompany it. It's the time I'll lose farther along the trail. A couple of weeks from now, standing on a mountaintop in the Sierras, I'll feel inspired. Or in Santiago, contemplating the cobblestones where a million pilgrims from 1,200 years have walked as I have, heart and soul will know the spirituality and peace I seek. These are inner things I want most from my trip. A problem with some kind of ailment on the front end means less time farther along when I hope I've been moved. I can always take a bus to make up lost time, and that's a fallback strategy. However, it too is something I want to avoid. I want to walk the whole country, carry my pack across every step, and experience all that might find its way onto my path.

This is part of my pilgrimage definition. I have to trust my journey will unfold the way it should, not necessarily the way I foresee it—lack of preparation, delays, or other issues notwithstanding. Camino forums speak widely of this, of being open to letting the experience be and not carry expectations. It's easy to say, but psychologically, I'm finding it hard to accomplish as I prepare for this second adventure. A week or so from now, my hope is to have this behind me. But at the moment, along with my sleeping bag and other odds and ends, I seem to be loading unseen expectations into my backpack accompanying other paraphernalia truly needed for the road.

I hope when I see the Pyrenees under my feet, I won't have further use for the expectations.

Encounters of the spiritual, the mysterious, I hope to experience on the trail across Spain again on this second journey. I likened them to a soft tap on the shoulder when attention had wandered, as it did most hours of most days in 2003. Walking created the meditative state, opened my heart, and slowed me sufficiently to appreciate things I might otherwise miss. These are things that appeared unimportant at first glance, but a moment later can reach inside and move profoundly. The often quiet time on the road unearthed my inner voice, pointed the way to many of these experiences. In a busy world, I rarely hear the voice, heed it even less. Trekking the Camino, this inner persona was permitted to take the lead.

I describe the sensation as awakening a new sense of trust within me.

On one occasion, I shared a glass of wine with a trekker who walked in 2003 because his doctor said he might not live to see 2004. My heart stopped when his words landed on our tiny table, realizing how casually I accept the blessing of good health. Though human in nature, such encounters touched deeper than mere words convey and presented a very spiritual moment.

Other encounters I found seemed more mystical. I remember a simple church that stood alone in the middle of a field. Eight hundred-year-old St. Mary of Eunates was apparently employed for the burial of pilgrims from the Middle Ages when severe illness and banditry were often fatal risks to pilgrim travel. St. Mary's is known to trekkers, but it's off the Camino path, requiring an hour's detour—two hours out and back. Walking such a side trip is not done lightly with sore feet or tired legs. Yet with no understanding of why, I knew in 2003 I should make the turn to go.

I remember the music of Zamphir was barely audible, the near-silence immediately powerful when I entered the church. It felt beyond peaceful, moving toward a sense of the sacred. I found a dozen other pilgrims settled in various pews when I arrived that day. Rain had literally thudded down through the morning, the sounds of a Spanish monsoon through the open door somehow harmonic accompaniment for the flute. For all its volume, rain seemed integral to the consuming ambiance. A blissful inner peace permeated the ancient structure and touched my heart without anything more obvious than its simple presence.

Perhaps it was the spirit of pilgrims past; perhaps it was the sacred. I came to understand a different sense of pilgrimage during my short stay. Eunates reminds of the history when people risked their lives for such experience; it underscored faith in the sacred and made me think of mine. Whether it was this I felt or the caress of a centuries-old building, soft beautiful music, or perhaps a combination of all, every person within the church was moved by moments spent at St. Mary's. The collection of international travelers, me included, each displayed tears on their faces, emotionally struck by something in the church. I wondered how many thought they were being touched by God.

I wondered if I was.

The experience felt as I might imagine the touch of God—gentle and loving and warming beyond description. I spoke to no one for a long while after I walked away from the 800 year old church. I wanted to hold the moment for as long as possible.

My hope of the coming month is for a re-acquaintance with such encounters.

TO BRING OR NOT TO BRING?

As the last days at home count down to zero, the "bring/don't bring" decisions on my mind are not of the sock-and-underwear variety. They are of precious items, which, despite the weight they might add, will lift me on the coming sojourn. I think I have my list:

> Sandra's scallop shell. The scallop is an icon of the Camino reputed to have been used to scoop from ponds or water wells before the modern era of camelbacks and plastic bottles. Many walkers acquire a shell somewhere en route for a couple of bucks and then attach it to dangle from their backpack along the Way of St. James. My wife and I each bought one in St. Jean Pied de Port on our original walk. For 2009, Sandra's 2003 version is on my pack.
>
> A teddy bear named Mikie. We lost my brother-in-law, Michael, to cancer a few months ago after an amazing ten-year battle. He was sixty-six and for thirty years was as much a brother as my own. I miss his wisdom already, his wit, laughter, friendship, and the love he had for my sister and so many others. I was lucky to be one of those others. He was a beautiful man, the kind who inspires

every day. I want Mikie to ride across Spain with me.

An electronic tape recorder. Small, light, and without a connection to the outside world, I hope it will at some point hold worthy thoughts and maybe save moments of inspiration.

A missal. Many of the churches across Spain are Catholic. The Catholic masses are universal, which is to say the same biblical passages are read in every church everywhere in the world on any given day. I can't speak Spanish, but this little booklet in English contains all the daily readings of the masses for September. When I do wander into a church, I can follow what's being said and read. I'm hoping the readings might speak to me.

No Netbook or Blackberry. These made the "don't bring" list. I expect a severe case of technology withdrawal, and maybe even the shakes for a few days, but these puppies need to stay home. I may regret it, but I think it's is the right decision. I was generously filled by quiet, tranquility, peace, and an almost constant meditative mode last time out. The combination supplied base elements for many experiences, encounters that moved my spirit. Internet cafes, phone cards, and pay phones will be my alternate. It will be so 1980s...

A bag of rocks. I know; this one's a little weird, especially on a journey where dumping weight is the prime directive. And to make it worse, I can't tell you what they're for. Not yet. Maybe in a few days.

T-MINUS ONE-DAY ANXIETY

I'm excited—so much so I wake earlier each day, eyes jolting open, mind running in overdrive. Less than twenty-four hours from now, I'll be over the Atlantic, so anticipation is driving everything faster. Have I got everything? Have I done everything? Am I ready?

I'm a little nervous.

I've got a couple of blisters on top of my big toes from the training regimen. Nothing serious, but it reminds me there wasn't really time to prepare as I might have liked. There may be more physical challenges ahead, but I'm hoping against it.

The weight of my pack is too great as someone noted, and I'll diligently work to get it down. If not, I'll shed pounds in Spain by mailing unnecessary items ahead to General Delivery at Santiago and pick them up when I arrive. A trick of the trade...

I leave my family, home, and other aspects of regular life arranged as best I can, but five weeks is a long time to be absent. I pray all stays well and the Lord looks after the management of things close to my heart.

My greatest anxiety surrounds expectation. I blogged about the ideal and I hoped to be going without any expectations. Unfortunately I've not succeeded. There were amazing experiences last time around, and I'm unable to empty my head of anticipation; hoping for similar moving, touching adventures. Worst still, as departure has drawn closer the problem has grown. I'm pretty sure without correction this is the road to disappointment.

A wise friend proposed a way out of my conundrum, and I'm going to give that a go. It involves the bag of rocks, but more on that later.

Tomorrow I walk out the front door and walk to the airport. It's traditional to start a pilgrimage in such a manner, from home, and it's a curiously exhilarating part of the experience. The local airport is such a familiar place for business trips and vacation starts, meeting family and seeing off friends—the journey to and fro always done by car. There aren't even sidewalks on the road to the terminal; so rare is it for someone to walk there. But it helped launch me last time; changing my mind set literally the moment I left home. I'm already feeling a buzz again. It's going to be different, though. Sandra is walking me to the airport, and at the gate, we'll part for over a month—the longest gap in our history. It's going to be hard to say good-bye and climb on the plane alone. Not sure how the schedule is going to go tomorrow. I may not be able to post, so I'll be back here in a day or two. The same is my plan for the entire walk. I'd like to post each day, but Internet cafés may not be available every day.

AIRPORT DAY

My pack is ten kilos/twenty-two pounds. I've battled excess pack weight and beaten it down. But my backpack still seems bloody heavy. I've gotten weaker with age.

This morning was my weekly men's breakfast club gathering—a group I've met over the last ten or so years. To a man, they are fine individuals. I am privileged to call them friends and supportive travelers of my life, my larger journey, and my faith.

I've attached Mikie, the teddy bear, on my backpack. I'm excited launch day is here and saddened to be leaving my home for so long. The mix seems a little numbing, as though the emotions are cancelling each other. As I ask myself how I feel, there doesn't seem to be a solid answer. I imagine Christopher Columbus may have sensed a bit of this sailing for America. The promise, hope, and adventure of a journey to seek a new and worthy place; apprehension about what it might do to him—perhaps challenge how he perceives the world and what he believes. My voyage is none so dramatic, but writing this last morning before leaving, surrounded by my personal life—Sandra; our home; our dog, Shelby—I have my own apprehension about how this journey might affect me. A lot has happened this year to make the walk significant.

The death of Michael, my-brother-in-law, was very hard, deeply painful. My eighty-eight-year-old mother is aging noticeably and growing more vulnerable. A couple of other life challenges have called for introspection. These, the economy bashing my financial world, and departing a job of four years produced sizeable shifting of my personal planet. The combination has created questions for me. I've always said I trusted God with my future. I realized, under the light of this year, I offered this trust as long as I felt I was really in control of my circumstances.

No one ever has that kind of control, but I convinced myself I had. So it wasn't perhaps real trust in God, just the appearance of it. This year there has been no control, so I've been trying on genuine trust to see how it fits. I'm finding it a little snug. I really have little to complain about in my life. There are people I love and who love me as I am, warts and all. I have my health. I'm not financially independent, especially with the market battering, but middle-class life treats me well enough. There is much to appreciate and little justification for complaint against these measures. Yet the year has brought a time of life's larger tribulations, bringing with it questions I haven't asked before, the path suggesting changes are afoot. My humanity feels the struggle.

I will have five weeks alone with my thoughts. It's a long time for me to be with just me. My younger sister was visiting this week and said it best: "It's about really going deep for a short while." I see not the destination, though, and even the direction of it is not fully defined. And there's the expectation creeping in again. Maybe I'm just going for a long walk in the country. A couple of hours now, trekking poles in hand, I'm out the door, down my street, and walking off to the airport. My honey will be walking with me for the ninety minutes or so it will take to dodge traffic and arrive alive.

Then I'm on my own.

MADE IT—SORT OF

August 29–30

It's 2:00 a.m., Sunday, in Pamplona. I made it, but I'm so excited I can't sleep. It's been a long thirty-six hours.

Friday, just after lunch, I closed my laptop and held the power button on my Blackberry long enough for the screen to go black. I don't expect to turn on either for thirty-five days. I anticipated panic would result from shutdown; I even had wine on standby as a sedative. But instead I was calm, the shutdown anticlimactic. I hadn't expected that. The anxiety of the previous twenty-four hours was somehow purged by powering down. The time had arrived, and ready or not, I was off. I felt ready. I had the wine anyway. And Sandra walked me to the airport.

I won't drive a car for the next month or face traffic congestion. Now in Spain, for me there are no planes, no trains, no buses, only the most basic of accommodations—foot travel—and almost zero modern world save for this blog. TV and newspapers are in Spanish, of which I understand almost none. I feel strange, even odd, a proverbial fish out of water. But I still feel calm. I realize the Camino is not only about going to another place; in a very real sense, it's about going to another time in history. There are tech products on my feet and back, trekking poles, and so on. But much else on my journey is as it was hundreds of years ago. I think this is part of the peaceful sense I have when I'm here. I feel a kinship with pilgrims of old.

I had a hard day getting here, though, and plans changed as a result.

Every now and then, I have one of those trips where the travel gremlins come out en masse. I don't mean a late flight or delayed baggage type of trip. I mean the kind where one thing after another after another requires a serious fight to get anything done. Well, such was my day getting to Pamplona, with events conspiring to slow my arrival, make the trip exasperating. I rented a car for the Madrid-Pamplona hop, thinking I could get here before the last bus left heading east to the Pyrenees. I got lost on my way out of Madrid. I never get lost. Really. Ask Sandra. Okay, almost never. But this was a doozy. I tacked over an hour onto the drive north, arriving just in time to miss that last bus. I couldn't get the rental car back to its rightful owners, then found there's no bus service to Pyrenees tomorrow, Sunday, and none at all to St. Jean Pied de Port. Half a dozen other incidents followed and I felt like running away for a time. Nothing seemed to be coming together.

Then I found Marta, a handsome, thirty-something desk clerk at the Leyre Hotel. Camino angels, Sandra and I called them last time. This one helped solve the car problem, then two other issues, mostly by being exceptionally kind, knowledgeable, and English-speaking. Foreign language is great entertainment when all is well, miserable when things are rough. Eventually, I decided I needed a night to recoup balance, maybe settle a little chi. The Leyre Hotel proved an oasis. Down the street I found a tapas bar, a cold beer, and a great bartender. His English and my pantomime interacted with ease, coordinating a delicious Saturday evening to close my otherwise bumpy day. I survived.

I did stop into the refugio near the cathedral where I found the backpack crowd, fellow pilgrims I've come to walk beside. I spoke to a couple of German fellows who invited me out and a Canadian woman from Vancouver who's trekking with a friend. They're here, these travelers from everywhere, and tomorrow I join their ranks, though I'm still a few hours from my outset.

This brings me to the change of plans.

I've struggled unsuccessfully for a lot of hours, trying to get east of Pamplona, into the Pyrenees Mountains. The harder I try, the more events resisted logistics and emotions became more frustrated. Late Saturday, with a little help from Sandra, I considered the subtext of the day. We always said the way to do the Camino is to just walk what's in front of you. No more, no less, and don't try to manage the outcome. Trust in what's happening. I can stay in Pamplona and continue the struggle, with the best result being my Camino won't start for a couple of days. Or I can face west and walk from here. I said on this blog a few days ago I would try to accept whatever the road has in store for me. Jumping in at Pamplona rather than a more easterly point seems to be a direction to me. I'm trying to listen. So tomorrow, I'm westbound, the distance to Santiago shortened by two and a half days, St. Jean to Pamplona. I'll see what the road holds tomorrow.

And the bag of rocks?

I've worried for a while now that expectations from the last Camino might stand in the way of this one. A friend told me that Buddhist monks occasionally collect rocks when faced with the same situation. Labeling each with a specific expectation, they carry the rocks until such time as they can discard the weight, both physical and emotional. This struck me as a useful approach, and so collected nine thumbnail sized stones, five labeled for moving spiritual events from my last walk and four belonging to emotions for this one. Sandra added one to the bag as well. I was expecting to drop the set of five one-by-one at the locations where the events occurred last time. A curious result of this day's frustration is that I feel comfortable letting go of all five rocks now. I've decided this walk is already unique, so I'll scatter the rocks as I walk away from Pamplona. My other four and Sandra's one have a distance to go.

AUGUST 30TH AND STILL TRYING

So I'm at the starting line, the engine's revving like mad, my shoulders are hunched in anticipation; I'm ready to *go*...

Not.

I can't get it into gear...

Ever see one of those movies where the lead actor is having a conversation or something similar, and as he turns to leave, the camera stays focused on the room while our star exits stage right? The zoom starts immediately, closer, closer, closer, until it pinpoints the forgotten bag of critical documents left on the desk, counter, or, in my case, the top of the pay phone at the refugio. Tension mounts as consequences are felt. The stage is set for problems and some serious swearing. I managed my loss during Saturday evening's brief visit to the local refugio, only discovering the absence of my documents this a.m. as I packed to leave the hotel where I stayed. In the Ziploc bag was my credencial, a small booklet utilized as a Camino passport of sorts, along with a special outline map of the trail. The map I can manage without—not so the credencial. It's my access pass to other refugios along the path, identifying me as a pilgrim, a user of the refugio facilities. Heavy sigh...

The refugio in Pamplona closes at 8:00 a.m. each day, sweeping the last of late rising walkers on their way to the next village west, reopening mid-afternoon to allow incoming from the east. It is only then can I hope to recover the missing docs. Another heavy sigh... I've not joined the pilgrim community; still feel like I'm looking in through the glass and, for some reason, not yet allowed to enter.

St. Jean Pied de Port, where I began last time, is an ancient town, the high-walled perimeter fortification giving it an authentic look of the medieval. Within the walls, centuries-old buildings tell of history, standing shoulder to shoulder along narrow cobblestone streets barely wide enough to accommodate foot traffic. The town is small, with perhaps a few thousand inhabitants. In the old city centre, shaven-haired, backpack-laden travelers are obvious. Most days, some fifty to seventy-five wander about for a single night's stay, awaiting the early morning commencement of a strange journey. Would-be pilgrims number well among locals, their presence apparent for anyone who cares to look. Last time I walked, largely because I felt I belonged to the fraternity of wanderers, the simple act of arrival in St. Jean was enough to emotionally establish my Camino. I remember my heart jumping when I entered the town, seeing these fellow pilgrims walking the streets. It's not the same this time.

Pamplona, famous for the running of the bulls, is closer to two thousand years in age, and in every way, it feels like walking the pages of history. Buildings are of times I studied in school, architecture Romanesque and baroque. To walk its streets is for me to imagine famous knights and kings, the real and the fictional. But Pamplona is much larger than St. Jean, with tens of thousands of residents, the number increased substantially by tourists, mostly of the non-backpacking variety. Pilgrims are an invisible minority here. So it would appear I am to remain separated from my desires, or at least to feel so, until mid-afternoon. I can then access the refugio and hopefully recover the missing credencial. Until then, I will continue to feel my Camino is just out of reach.

I wondered about God in this circumstance.

I have never believed God the cause of hardship nor pain. So I don't believe God "caused" any of the difficulties that have swirled about for the last two days. But I sense God may be pleased events are unfolding as they are. I continue to experience a different and difficult start to my journey. And while it's frustrating to no end, I am slowing emotionally, and I sense expectations are being purged. There is no "real" hardship to events so far, but mind and attitude shifts are definitely underway. I arrived in Spain with my plan set out of how I would walk, where I would start, and how I would feel as the journey's first days of mountain scenery unfolded. All are now gone. As agitated as I was this morning at the delay and then discovering the missing credencial, I'm now okay about hanging around Pamplona another day. There's a midday service at the cathedral I can take in—an inspiring way to begin my walk, even take my first steps. I'm going to sit in the plaza mayor this afternoon, watch multigenerational Spanish families come and go, keep my feet up, and drink a cold beer under the rays of what looks to be a glorious day. I feel a greater calm taking hold within as I write these words. I'll check into the refugio this day, sleep among fellow walkers tonight, listen to stories of the Pyrenees I will not see. And tomorrow, an hour or so before daybreak, I'll rise with my family of pilgrims and start anew.

One day at a time. Trust in what's before me.

This could be a fine way to start.

Thank you, God. I don't understand how things unfold in the universe, but this day, I sense your touch on the warm feeling I'm experiencing.

AUGUST 30TH: PART II

It's finally together in Spain. The sun is shining hot on the town square, tapas and drinks have filled my belly, and yes, I've landed at the local hostel refugio. Credencial and Ziploc are safely within my pack. The Leyre Hotel has been traded out for the chatter of a hundred or more Germans, Dutch, Americans, Aussies, Brits, and others. It's busy—the hubbub of Camino refugio life a familiar sound—check-in, locate a bed, daily clothes washing, introductions, and story sharing. It stands in sharp contrast to the isolation I felt last night, despite the comfort of a modern hotel. I can now feel the embrace of fellow travelers. I'm not alone.

Blogging time and Internet cafés may be less frequent as I head forward, but I hope not. Circumstances have provided generous opportunity here in Pamplona, but tomorrow, I walk. I'll return soon.

ON THE ROAD AGAIN

The ramparts of Pamplona are eleven hours to my back; forty-three kilometers (almost twenty-five miles) have passed underfoot since yesterday morning. It took eight hours to cover yesterday's distance, another three so far today. In my other world, eleven hours in a plane could see me from Toronto to Tel Aviv, in a car get me from Washington, DC, to the middle of Florida. Eleven hours of walking in America would be more than enough to get me from downtown Manhattan to the outer most edge of New York City. I love the comparison.

My Camino memory and my new journey seem to be coming into balance. Now with familiar scenery passing slowly by, I remember much from before, and the remnants of expectations are further diminished.

Yesterday's walk was done under a clear blue sky, many liters of water required to offset fluids lost to the heat of the day. It was threatening 30C most of the time, close to 90F. My destination was Cirauqui, a hilltop village of terracotta and sandstone-colored buildings, the red tile roofs and matching cobblestone streets, a postcard for Spanish travel. A five hundred-year-old weatherworn stone church crowns the peak in the town, my tiny albergue accommodation on the main square sitting opposite its bell tower. I arrived just in time. The last twenty minutes of the walk required all the energy that remained in me, the short climb to the top of the hill much tougher than it might have been earlier in the day. I was completely spent physically at the crest, my emotions on a serious high for completing the task. I did it. I did it. I did it. I've returned to the Camino de Santiago, and my first day feels awesome.

I can't properly describe how fabulous a shower feels after such a huge effort, dry clothes from my pack a treasure to slip into. After complete physical exhaustion to make the distance, the simple act of fresh water and fresh clothes are like heaven. A huge plate of spaghetti and meatballs, preceded by fresh baguettes, homemade soup, a bottomless jug of wine, and a simple dessert were equally amazing. An ancient wine cellar beneath the inn where I stayed was an unexpected and spectacular place to dine. It was a ten. The dinner fabulously prepared, my effort spent to get to it enhancing each mouthful.

I met the youngest pilgrim ever yesterday, eight-month-old Oliver. Anders and Elizabeth, his Norwegian parents, were pushing the toddler across two weeks of Camino, skipping only the areas of trail too steep or too rough for their off-road-style baby buggy. The miniature carriage was equipped to carry one of their backpacks, the second on the back of one parent or the other. Oliver, the buggy, and a single-loaded pack apparently came in at 60 kilos, about 130-odd pounds. I can't imagine pushing such a weight halfway across Spain. It was inspiring to listen to the parents; both were so full of life and couldn't wait for today to walk again. Oliver, clearly enjoying himself, was passed from one adult to another during dinner, giggling his way around the room as he went. I found myself wondering if I could be as brave to undertake that complex a family outing with such a young child. The baby enhanced the feeling of fraternity and family I felt throughout the evening. The boisterous laughter of fellow travelers, with Oliver's distinctive little laugh mingled in, reminded me of growing up many years ago. Our family home back then, with seven siblings, was much the same. The hardship and sweat of the road forgotten, the night may turn out to be a very memorable evening of my new Camino.

 I walked for much of the day with Jill, a psychotherapist from Britain. A midfifties woman, she's been winding down her practice for a year to take a sabbatical. Her Camino planning started in February, and last week, she departed her husband and family for five weeks on the road alone. We met at the cathedral in Pamplona during a brief ceremony for the blessing of the pilgrims. This pilgrims' blessing happens every evening and draws almost all travelers passing through. Delivered entirely in Spanish, it's impossible to understand what's going on without the language. Despite this, it is a tradition of walkers to seek the blessing, whether traveling for spiritual reasons or simply for an adventure hike. It is important for all, rare to find someone missing in the pews.

I came across this English version of the Pilgrim's prayer shortly after my first walk:

> *Lord, you who recalled your servant Abraham out of the town Ur in Chaldea and who watched over him during all his wanderings; you who guided the Jewish people through the desert; we also query to watch your present servants, who for love for your name, make a pilgrimage to Santiago de Compostela.*
>
> *Be for us,*
> *A companion on the journey*
> *The guide on the intersections*
> *The strengthening during fatigue*
> *The fortress in danger*
> *The resource on our itinerary*
> *The shadow in the heat*
> *The light in the darkness*
> *The consultation during dejection*
> *And the power of our intention*

> *So that we under your guidance, safely and unhurt, may reach the end of our journey and strengthened with gratitude and power, secure and filled with happiness, may join our home. For Jesus Christ, our Lord. Amen.*
>
> *Apostle James, pray for us*
> *Holy Virgin, pray for us*
> *Our Lady of the Pillar, pray for us.*

Jill has been a great travel companion, sharing very personal stories, her life experiences fascinating to hear. I realized I relish this type of encounter. Sharing personal stories with someone I've just met is not something I do easily or often. Naturally reserved, I take time to know someone, careful that any sharing doesn't move beyond my knowledge and control of where the information might go. Here on the road, there's no likelihood of a surprise. I know it, and so do others. The result for me is a rare comfort to be completely open when I find someone I connect with emotionally, and the posture is usually reciprocated. It suits my sense of the ideal, being so candid with someone I've just met. Good and possibly great friendships, something I find harder to establish as years go by, are easily nurtured along the trail in Spain. I remember a few from the last walk; maybe I have a new one starting on this walk.

Following the same path, I'm meeting the fraternity of pilgrims, time spent walking, in refugios, and over dinners, providing many opportunities to meet and connect. I find much hope for these connections and possibly something deeper and more personal for the coming weeks.

I'm a pilgrim again.

AN AUSSIE

He needed a poke with a sharp stick...

Four hours into the day, under the strain of a long hill climb and unrelenting afternoon sun, I was sweating myself dry. Anthony didn't have a single bead running down his forehead, while I was soaked from forehead to waist band. Jill is still with me, she and I walking with the physiotherapist from down under on and off for most of this morning and yesterday afternoon. In his midthirties, Anthony is interesting, pleasant, and very fit. Well into my second day, I was struggling to make my last hour's walk when Anthony reached back to grab his pack with both hands and left me in his dust. The Aussie set off in a jog toward the next town. It was depressing to see so much energy still on tap while I was pretty sure I was dying. If he did it again, I decided I was going to throw my trekking poles at him...

I have been wondering how to interpret this walk, my drawing health care professionals as fellow travelers. After very little thought, I've decided that at least one benefit is the opportunity to have a mental or physical breakdown during my Camino with complete assurance I'll be in good hands...

So we are three in regular contact, on and off over the last while, now on our way through Logroño. Thirty-six hours over the past three and half days have seen me to this bustling city one hundred kilometers west of Pamplona. An hour on an intercity bus would carry me all the way back. Travel has proven long and exhausting, each day's final mile or so an endurance test with strength and stamina waning. Satisfaction trumps, though, when I tumble spent but still smiling into my chosen overnight stop. The rest stops have each been a gem so far.

On Tuesday, it was a refugio run by Dutch evangelicals. I was nervous about the possibility of too much religious fervor, but it was not the case. The small group hosted some twenty-five *peregrinos,* the Spanish word for pilgrims, with soft spiritual infusion. We said grace before a fabulous dinner that had been cooked by our Dutch hosts, were offered a booklet of the Gospel of John only if it was wanted, and later invited to a thirty-minute meditation. The meditation was attended by half the travelers and included a reading of King David's psalm. I was very impressed and very comfortable—something in all honesty I hadn't expected. I like the way spirituality seems to surface on this journey. It doesn't often arrive in traditional or obvious manner; instead, it seems to enter my days in unexpected ways. The mediation with the Dutch high up in the hillside village, the blessing of the pilgrims in Pamplona, a quiet evening mass stumbled upon at Cirauqui, angelic hymns playing softly in the frighteningly high choir loft of an eleventh-century church. This last one was hauntingly beautiful, despite my fear of heights. I sat in blissful peace for the time we gathered in the darkened loft. The encounters are most welcome, intrinsic for me to the spirit of Camino, and meld into my walk without my seeking them. They land as food for my soul. I like it.

I feel greatly touched as well by some of the people of Spain I come across.

A day or two ago—the days seem to blend one into the other already—I climbed a several hundred-meter rise, well more than a thousand feet over an hour's trek. The next town still forty-five minutes away, some fellow had driven a pint-sized minivan to the crest of the rise, serving hot coffee, cold drinks, and energy bars to sweaty pilgrims. His prices were some of the lowest I've seen, and I suspect revenues would barely cover his food costs and gas but definitely not the vehicle. Yet there he was, parked ten miles from nowhere simply to offer a brief but very-needed respite to a band of international walkers, none of whom he will ever see again. It's inspiring and humbling to experience such generosity from a stranger. The gestures move me deep inside.

The journey continues. Logroño marks six hundred kilometers remaining to Santiago.

A MINOR CORRECTION

Okay, maybe I shouldn't have left all my technology at home; a calculator clearly seems to be in order. Earlier in the blog, I said I had been traveling for 3.5 days and 36 hours. Not so. Must have been my enthusiasm. Three and a half days was correct, but each day is around 8 hours. So the math was more like 25 hours. But it's a moot point, as day six is now over, offering a claim of near 45 hours, 160 kilometers, or 100 miles—a distance which took twice that number of days during training.

I was seriously anxious about Spain with so little preparation. I've been reluctant to report on how I've been holding up, great believer that I am that Murphy and his laws can strike as soon as the "all's well" has been issued. But all is well. Nothing has fallen off, there are no blisters, and days are managed better than expected, especially for the first week. The end of each daily segment still brings exhaustion, an average thirty kilometers (almost twenty miles) traveled during the eight hours. Feet are sore from the continuous foot pounding, gravel trails, or pavement hastening discomfort; grass and dirt are much preferred. Back muscles ache, unaccustomed as I am to the pack weight. But the mid-afternoon shower, hot or cold, and clean clothes bring surprisingly rapid rejuvenation. A half hour's lie down after daily laundry, and my recovery is nearing 80 percent. By morning, I'm not only ready to go again but excited to be underway. I start the days happy to be here, feeling especially privileged for this opportunity. Even in the late day, fatigued and dragging the last steps into a refugio, I still find reason to smile. I'm doing it a lot... smiling, not dragging. If all stays in check, the days should become a little easier with more travel and time. I don't expect I'll ever feel like jogging after ending my day but less like collapsing is something to look forward to...

I've been staying in smaller refugios, in smaller villages. This decision means fewer people at the overnight rest stops and fewer opportunities to connect during the day when varied walking speeds disperse fellow pilgrims significantly along the length of the day. It translates into more time alone, hours without sight of others. It feels great most of the time to have such personal space, but occasionally a long stretch of trail ahead brings a feeling of isolation, even loneliness can creep in. It's brief, but it happens. I treat it as part of the journey.

The upside of the small refugios is people—those who operate the places I stay, and those who visit as pilgrims. Hospitaleros, keepers of the refugio inns, seem more personal in the less populated villages, and dinner involves home-cooked meals. Mealtime tables for eight, ten, or twelve bring noisy chatter of home countries and road stories, usually continuing outside in the later evening and occasionally running on at rest stops the following day. Conversations provide surprisingly private and moving stories between pilgrims, the open, candid nature of walkers increasing as days multiply.

Jill, my psychotherapist from London, is still walking close by off and on. We are together for a few hours, then one stops for something, the other continuing on. I expect we'll lose contact at some point, possibly reconnect a few weeks later in Santiago at the end of the journey. Anthony, the Aussie physiotherapist, succumbed to a substantial round of blisters, took a day off, and has disappeared behind me. Francois, a sixty-something doctor from Paris, has been in the same refugios as me for several overnights. We travel together occasionally by day. She and her husband walked the Camino many years ago and promised each other they would do it again someday. His passing a year ago left the commitment unfulfilled. Francois determined shortly after his death to do the walk for them both, giving up on a first attempt when the emotional struggle proved too great. She returned two weeks ago to try again. Francois travels quietly, with enormous strength and determination. I take great inspiration simply watching her walk.

I met an older man, Shawn, and his adult son, Killean, a few days ago, the two coming from Connemara, Ireland. The brogue on them both is so thick, at times, I can't understand their words, and I'm Irish. We spent an evening together, sitting again the next day over a ten-minute coffee stop that took an hour. Shawn explained, in typical Irish-storytelling style, his five children had been born with just one year between each. He says when he finally discovered what was causing the new arrivals, he swore to avoid the cause for ever more. Shawn's delivery is so subtle I almost wiped out the table, laughing at his punch line. His beautiful heart and sharp, easy wit reminded me of my own father. The feeling made me wish morning coffee could last all day. Shawn is walking a portion of the Camino, health limiting his days to short distances. Next year, he intends to return to cover another section, then to be accompanied by another of his children. The remaining three he hopes will walk with him in subsequent years. Shawn's hope is a family experience, done one by one, becoming a journey for him to share with all his children.

Today, I spent time with two American women, Lindsay and Christine, from California. The twenty-somethings quit respective jobs, Christine to walk the Camino and investigate Spain as a place to live and work. Lindsay is in

Spain to support her friend for both tasks, then heading back to America in November. Their voices resound with great friendship and great adventure. I loved listening to them.

Hope and optimism, smiles and struggle—all are present, all carried some distance to Santiago. I find it easy to become emotional listening to stories so generously imparted and offering some of my own in return. It feels big, seemingly nothing guarded, all real and honest. I feel part of my own journey in some of the conversations others share and know I'm not alone on either the Camino de Santiago or the Camino of my life.

WEEK ONE

It's official—I'm getting a complex. I've acquired another Aussie health care professional, this one a psychiatrist. Clearly I'm here for my mental health.

And I've discovered another issue. Walking west eight hours a day, the sun to the south, I'm getting a great tan on my left leg, left arm, and the left side of my face. But my right leg, arm, and face, turned for most of the day away from the sun, remain pale and anemic-looking. I've thought of walking backward for a few hours each day, but somehow that kind of vanity I'm supposed to give up on a pilgrimage. So I'm putting up with this terrible hardship...

There have been a few other items of difficulty during my first seven days; I left my soap behind at the first refugio, a critical item given the amount of sweat involved with walking a loaded backpack across the country. Then I did it again two days later with the replacement soap—clearly I'm trying to avoid washing chores. On the subject of washing, I managed to forget that my digital voice recorder was in one of the seventeen pockets of my cargo pants. It went for forty minutes in the wash and rinse before eight hundred revolutions in the spin cycle. My journal notes are on the little device. I stared at the blank screen for two days, saying lots of prayers for its recovery.

The tiny contraption came back to life yesterday intact, operational, and with all my previous notes. You guys at Olympus make great technology, and I promise not to wash the little device again. Finally, there was the wrong turn Wednesday. It added an hour to the end of the day when feet really weren't interested in traveling any farther. But I'm alive and well otherwise.

Mikie is traveling well. I'm often asked why there's a teddy bear riding on my backpack. I love to tell fellow pilgrims of Michael and the special person my brother-in-law was. It's emotional at times to talk about him, his passing still so recent and so hard. Yesterday, I passed a Brazilian on the trail. As I moved away, she called "Buen Camino, Mikie" after me. The salutation brought tears.

I'm traveling for my eighth day now, 60 hours on the trail, 210 kilometers, or 125 miles behind me as I arrive in Burgos. I met, dined, and bunked with over 200 different people from some 24 different countries. Over the days I've met Americans, Canadians, people from most European countries, Brazil, New Zealand, Australia, and a couple of others are in the mix beyond these. Between walking, mealtimes, and resting, there have been several dozen deeply personal, intimate conversations. Dinners in out-of-the-way refugios have been like family affairs—the smallest with eight sharing bread, and the largest found twenty-four sitting at one long table. At this last one, several of us had collectively helped to prepare supper, then waited as simmering aromas wafted about the rustic house with two dozen pilgrims famished from a long day's trek. In the end, it was a most satisfying time, with plenty to reach for seconds.

Everyone I speak with, it seems, has an amazing story under the covers, a personal and sometimes poignant purpose behind their Camino. A few of these came out in a most unusual way the other night.

Following dinner with the twenty-four, we were invited to a small chapel in an attic-like room. I'm claustrophobic, so the low ceiling and three-foot-high door almost turned me away. I closed my eyes once inside and surprisingly found it comfortable to stay. Juan Jose and Anne Marie, hosts of the slanted, tired, spotless refugio in Tosantos, manage four languages between them: English, French, Spanish, and German. The two innkeepers had decided a few days before I arrived to ask the group of then-visiting pilgrims to write down their reasons for walking the eight hundred kilometers. Names were not to be provided, just the intention. Each of the pilgrims from that night wrote in one of the four languages common in the refugio. Juan Jose and Anne Marie committed to pray these intentions for twenty days, the time expected for the group to travel from Tosantos to their destination, Santiago de Compostela. To further support these intentions, Juan Jose and Anne Marie offered to ask the next twenty overnight groups to pray for them as well.

My night was a few days after the original group had passed through. During a meditation later in the evening, Juan Jose and Anne Marie shared this story and passed the basket of written intentions around the attic chapel, asking us each to draw one. English to English pilgrims, Spanish to Spanish, and so on was the only effort to control who received which intention. One by one, each of us read aloud in the inscribed language the intention we had drawn. I understood only a handful—the ones read in English. One asked to recover a faith lost many years before, one to grow nearer to God. Another of the English intentions asked for the ability to love and accept himself as he is, failings and all. Mine was from a man trying to rid himself of old habits and behaviors—obstacles, he had written—to grow closer in his relationships.

I'm fortunate to say I've never lost my faith, but the rest of the intentions fit some part of my life more than I liked. I prayed the next day for the intention I had read as Juan Jose and Anne Marie had asked and prayed as well for all the other intentions I bring from home. I was fascinated how I felt lifted by the evening events of the night before, lifted more the next day contemplating them. I talked to a few others along the path, faces I had seen in Tosantos, who revealed a similar experience. There was neither weight nor darkness to the intentions, mine or those of the others for whom we prayed. Rather there was a lightness to it all that somehow filtered through a rainbow of brightly colored emotions: love, kindness, humility, simplicity, generosity, humanness. It was hard not to smile. It was a big smile and lasted a long time.

Over coffee later in the day, chatting with one of my healthcare professionals, I realized I'm very pleased with myself. The feeling is not from smugness or righteousness. Instead, it's bound to a sense of gratitude, appreciation for this time, this place, this opportunity to simply walk. I'm doing great things for my body, the positive effects of one week already outwardly obvious, even with soreness present in the last hour of some days. I'm doing great things for my heart. I feel a rich, positive, fully alive sense of me seemingly all hours of all days. And I'm doing good things for my soul. These are not as easily described, but they come in the form of pilgrims blessings at churches and refugios, the smiles and waves of old Spaniards who know of the good of the Camino, and it comes from knowing the personal intentions of others, knowing my prayers help me and them as we walk toward the west one day at a time.

THE MESETAS BEGIN

Pictures, pictures, pictures—you'd think I'd have hundreds by now, posted in the photos section of this website or somewhere nearby. Well, you are practically correct. I have hundreds of pictures in the camera, but I'm desperately short of an accessible USB socket to upload. The sockets on most Internet café computers are locked off, presumably for fear of a virus. It's frustrating not having some way to share. Stay tuned, I'll find a means…

My first ten days across Spain have taken in the trailing foothills of the Pyrenees and the beautiful Rioja wine country of the northeast. Known the world over for excellent vintages, the trek carries through the countless vineyards, broad valleys, and gentle slopes of grapes ready to drop under their own weight. Harvest time is near. I've been blessed to sit on hilltops during walks for rest stops and for overnights to simply admire these vistas, timeless and beautiful. It has not been hard on the eyes. The city of Burgos signals a change in this terrain, the departure of Rioja vineyards. From Burgos, the Mesetas stretch westward—the next segment of the journey. I'm in Frómista, for those of you with really good maps. It's a little town two-days walk west of Burgos.

Eight hundred kilometers, five hundred miles, is not insurmountable, but it is unimaginable, at least at the outset. Even the second time around, it's hard to fathom. I noticed last time, and again this year, the first few days the question mostly commonly heard is: "Are you going to Santiago?"—destination city of the walk. And for those first days, the answer is yes. Several days of walking later, though, it becomes evident Santiago is too far to think about, too far to imagine. Twenty-five to thirty miles into the journey, the destination drops from conversations, and is replaced with "Where are you going today?" The only way to tackle the unimaginable is in pieces: eight hours; twenty-five kilometers; fifty miles; Punta la Reina, Burgos, or whatever the next town. A single-day's travel can be imagined, can be accomplished.

    This early change sets up a lovely mindset for me, living in the day, not worrying about tomorrow, not regretting yesterday. Tomorrow brings hot or cold, long or short, dust or calm. Anticipating it does nothing, changes nothing, and alters preparation not one bit. Yesterday was traveled as best I could, whether the hoped for destination was reached or an earlier stop needed. It's the way the Camino must be traveled. It reminds me of how to travel life, an approach I know well but rarely achieve. In Spain, though, for a month—a glorious thirty days—I live the ideal. Each day gets 100 percent of my physical and emotional energy, wasting nothing on past or future. I wish it were always so.

As for my regular companions, I've lost them. When I left Burgos well before sunrise, I headed out into central Spain. Jill, my British psychotherapist, stayed behind, opting for several shorter days to relieve her feet. June, the Aussie psychiatrist, has taken a bus forward a few days distance to relieve a time pressure for her travel plans. The other Aussie, Anthony, the physiotherapist, has been missing for days. So has the French doctor. So the plains of Spain begin alone for me.

It was great, the jokes and entertainment about having mental and physical health care specialists around all the time. In reality, I enjoyed the frequent company. For some reason, I was a little unsettled my first days on the Camino, perhaps a result of the frustrations getting started in Pamplona. It surprised me, as before arriving in Europe, I had been looking forward to experiencing wine country alone; the lovely scenery I expected to consume my attention and my days easily.

I expected the opposite heading into the sparser flatlands of central Spain, anticipated a desire for a companion or two during this coming segment. In the Mesetas, the mountains pull back to the distant horizons, the fields heave little, towns are farther apart. It supports the idea of being able to see forever. The effect is big sky country, intimidating enough for some to skip part or all eight to nine days needed to travel across the plain. On my previous journey, with Sandra by my side, I found the time introspective, a deep meditative mode resulting from the days spent there. Those who do walk speak similarly of the experience. The Mesetas are very manageable. Walking by myself this time, I expected to seek a Camino friend to face the crossing. Instead, I've walked the first two days alone and thoroughly enjoyed the time, pleased to have parted with my early travelers. I may see them later in the journey. For now, I love the quiet, walking the big country solo. There is no sense of being alone, and the stark beauty somehow suits me well. My meditation mode is returning.

    It's a great feeling.

FINGERPRINTS

Thank you for all the comments. I don't respond to everyone, but I definitely read them all. One asked what I consider the most significant moment of my trip so far.

Relaxing on the stone terrace of a five hundred-year-old villa perched in a hilltop village, catching the last of sunset on a Rioja wine valley is a spectacular moment. Feeling pleased I walked eight hours to get there, being fed a lovely meal, and enjoying the fruits of the valley was blissful, every sense telling me of a perfect moment.

Along the path, small towns have big churches; big towns have magnificent cathedrals. Services are conducted evenings, so a daytime visit finds beautiful silence within. Lights dimmed, sunrays cast beams through stained glass, the presence within an eight hundred-year-old holy building is penetrating. A great sense of awe pervades my inner core—some of it emotion, some imagination—thinking of others who sat where I sit a thousand lifetimes ago. I feel a deep peace in such places. There've been many moments like these.

The amazing people I've met, their stories, quaint and rustic refugios and albergues—there is a lot to choose from when I think of special moments.

There isn't one event to point out, but a type of event seems to touch me a lot. Here are a few examples.

I wasn't really aware of feeling off when I started out of Pamplona, wasn't looking for fellow travelers to sooth my spirit. They arrived unsolicited, becoming an integral and welcome part of my Camino. When I arrived in Burgos a week later, I was ready to continue alone, not sure how to suggest a separation from pilgrims who had become close friends. Without my mentioning this desire, each departed, each for a different reason. I was as I wanted to be. It appeared at first as good fortune, coincidental timing. However, as my journey unfolds, I find events such as these take on different context.

Spain is a late to bed, late to rise country—at least in the north where I travel. Leaving towns and villages a couple of hours before sunrise, nothing stirs, nothing moves. It is the same in the larger cities. I'm regularly awakened at 2:00–3:00 a.m. by revelers below my windows and then can't get coffee for love or money before 8:00 a.m. I was leaving a city very early a few days ago to put away some miles before sunrise and the heat of the day. It was a dreary trek out of the large centre. At the local university, road construction removed the Camino guide markers, leaving me lost with no way to determine my route to the country.

No other backpackers were to be seen in the still dark morning, and no traffic moved about.

During the thirty-minute trek to where the markers disappeared, I passed less than a handful of cars. Three minutes by the university roadside and a lone vehicle, a taxi passed; I'm dusty, backpack on the ground, fumbling with a map, obviously a lost pilgrim. The taxi brake lights came on immediately as he went by, turned, came back, and pulled to the curb in front of me. I expected to be seen as a possible fare. Instead, the driver came to the sidewalk, began to talk quickly in Spanish. To my good fortune, he did so with a lot of hand gestures, so I got the general idea of his words. Pointing to a road I wouldn't have taken, telling me keep to the right side, then a left, with a final zigzag out of town, the cabbie identified my needed route. He questioned my understanding with a universal "okay." I nodded, and he was gone before I could offer money. I found my way out of the city, didn't see another car after my encounter with the cab.

There are maps and guides to assist walkers, but it's possible to travel the Camino without. Yellow splashes of paint provide markers; arrows pointing the way across the country have been brushed on seemingly everything, everywhere. These are the markers I lost at the university. It can happen on rare occasions an arrow might be missing, faded from sun, or fallen to roadwork, as was my situation.

Monday, entering Burgos with another walker, I arrived at an intersection bearing no arrow. Three possible roads lay ahead, no obvious choice which to take. I stood for less than a few seconds when a whistling fellow with a bucket strolled by. He paused directly across the street, reached into the bucket, drew out a paintbrush, and vertically stroked the corner of a building. As he dabbed a matching yellow arrow on top, my fellow walker and I burst into laughter. The painter turned and smiled mischievously, offered a slight bow. I called across, "Muchas gracias, señor." His smile widened considerably. His reply: "Señor, non. Amigo, si. Amigo de peregrino. Amigo de Camino." Interestingly, just minutes earlier, my traveling companion asked if I thought there was a little man somewhere running around with a bucket of yellow paint splashing arrows on walls.

These were not the only such incidents, but as they mount in number, I get greater purpose from them, a special sense. There have been perhaps a dozen incidents like these since Pamplona, one of which was profoundly personal and moving. To me, frequency, timing, and their personal nature eliminate any sense of randomness. My inner voice—my spirit, perhaps—tells me there's more. My heart feels it, feels large. I don't think of these events as mystical—that's too substantial. But equally distant is coincidence. I've always thought of such experiences as somehow bearing the "fingerprints of God." They look and feel like what I might expect of his hand.

I don't know how such events come to be; God's direction perhaps, inspiration, angels, maybe something else. I do know these events feel as though they have been touched by the divine; they have a sense of his presence, his fingerprints. The experiences have a personal nature, particularly as I consider the precise timing and exact need they meet; these seem to be characteristics of "fingerprint events." I can offer no better explanation. In the quiet of my walk across Spain, my sense of spirituality is heightened. Perhaps away from the busyness of life, the multitasking of my world, I'm more attuned. I suspect fingerprint events occur as frequently at home as here, though I believe this environment, the history, and surroundings contribute much. Quiet, meditative, gentle, I feel a greater ability to recognize fingerprints when they find me.

It's not just the events that are special, though some clearly are. It has more to do with the resulting calm I experience; it lingers more with each event, penetrates gently, and makes the unfolding journey rich.

Over dinner in a sidewalk cafe my night in Burgos, a couple of other pilgrims and I shared opinions about these kind of events, they having experiences as well.

"Lovely coincidences," offered one.

"Synchronicity," said the second.

I answered, "Someone's looking after me."

WOMEN

I'm having another tanning crisis.

With shared and sometimes-crowded bathrooms, I decided shaving would be a luxury to leave at home. Twelve days in, there was substantial growth. Realist that I am, I thought I would look like one of those guys in magazines with the perfect five-day shadow. When I checked out the mirror, though, the image was more Grizzly Adams. That and specifically an annoying itch caused the razor to appear, hair now gone. However...the semi-beard concealed my chin from sunlight for almost two weeks, the underside now a pristine white. It doesn't match the bronze of my left cheek with its constant southern exposure nor the paler cheek on the north side of my face. I'm not sure what to call this look, but I don't think it's good. Fortunately, there's a sturdy clothes line outside. I'm thinking of hanging upside down with the freshly drying laundry to see if I can get just the right angle and maybe a bit of color under there...

The demographics of my Camino travelers in September 2009 are curious. Over one hundred thousand walked last year, the number consistently larger year over year. Men factor slightly more, but the split is fairly even across both genders. Until a few years ago, the Camino favored those over fifty. This line has flattened, age now being well represented from twenty-five to about seventy. There are exceptions; Juliette and Enrico are a couple of Italian students—she in second-year architecture, he in third-year history. She's a young Penelope Cruz lookalike; he equally able to capture admiring glances. Twenty-one and twenty-two respectively, they are trying to do something important—their words—to set the direction of their lives. Two weeks of walking, they giggle, laugh, talk, and support each other across the country. I also met a Danish couple walking for their third time. They rely on a support vehicle to carry backpacks but otherwise trek the same distance I do. She is seventy-nine; he's eighty-one. Both couples inspire me.

Each day between April and November, some fifty to one hundred people start the trek from each of St. Jean Pied de Port, Roncesvalles, and Pamplona. Most need about a month to make the eight hundred-kilometers, five hundred-mile journey across Spain. I'm in this category. Like many, I walk a little farther one day, a little less on another. This keeps me in a kind of three-day "wave of pilgrims," jumping between the block I started with, the travelers a day ahead or the one just behind. Some two hundred to three hundred people span the collection. Many faces are now familiar—some from across restaurants and overnight stops, and others from cafe conversations or chatting on the road. A few dozen have shared significant life events, with me reciprocating their confidence.

In any given wave, the demographics of age and gender swing, mine being something like 80 percent women, the majority around my age. Jill and June, each trekking solo, were my main companions week one. Since then, I've walked with Peggy, a fifty-year-old out-of-work artisan from Chicago, taking six weeks away from her job hunting to enjoy personal time. Diana and her friend, Rowena, are from my hometown. Diana walks with a constant smile, both feet badly blistered since day one. One of those effervescent type of people, somehow the enjoyment she gets from the walk overcomes any need to stop or quit. They travel with a striking blonde Italian woman who, along with the other two, seem to have formed a kind of female three musketeers of the Camino; they've become inseparable friends. Katherine and Anne are lifelong companions—one Swiss, one German. An uplifting couple, they constantly smile and joke with me as we move west. The two decided after twenty-five years of marriage their respective husbands could feed themselves for a few weeks and left to travel across Spain. They smiled mischievously describing the details of their escape. Katherine introduced Anne, pointing to charity work she does in her church and community. Katherine intended that she describe Anne as saintly, but the Swiss translation brought out the word *holy*. Anne was immediately christened "Holy Anne." She seems to love the title, raising both arms in girlish glee each time we connect, calling out "Holy Anne is here..." The two women have beautiful hearts. I love spending time with them, find myself hoping our cafe breaks or nighttime stops coincide. Muriel I walked with for just half a day. She lost her twenty-one-year-old son to a car accident four years ago. Piercing blue eyes and a soft face hide much of the journey she's on.

In one way or another, I share much with the feelings of each. I can't know the loss of a child, can't even imagine it. I have, though, lost people I love: my father; Sandra's mother, Amira; Michael. I reflect often on my life's journey of joy and struggle, friendships and the road I travel at home. I'm reminded of all as the Camino path unfolds, years I recall as yesterday. Memories support the sense of the kinship I experience here, my fellow pilgrims and I, paths that make our individual travel both similar and unique. Their hearts have touched mine and at times have reached my soul, those who travel the five hundred miles alone, some with a friend, some bearing great weight, some walking for reasons not yet clear to them. All are woven into the emotional fabric of my walk.

Of the men I've met, most are without English, me without a second language either. Three of the English-speaking men I have met are Peter, a vicar in a church north of London; Alan, the same in a church nearby; and Ralf, a priest at Westminster Abbey. When I figure out why my walking companions so far are exclusively women and the clergy, I'll report back. Meanwhile, I feel my company of pilgrims immensely special.

I've made it to León; some 325 kilometers, 200 miles, remain to Santiago. It's hard to fathom more miles now lay behind me than on the road ahead, stunning how fast the distance has fallen underfoot. It seemed an unimaginable distance a short while ago, yet the miles are consumed by time, each day a little more. Walking today, I realized the similarity to my life's journey. Turning fifty-five in 2009, two-thirds of my years are behind; time which once seemed infinite is now fleeting. The notion prompted more thoughts recent and long past of people in my life, those special to me. I found myself smiling unconsciously. I feel greatly blessed for them, my family, and friends—the ones I love. I've enjoyed my path, the decisions I've made, and the places where time has been spent. They've kept me moving in the right direction. Like this trail across Spain, there were places I didn't stay, choices given up, one in favor of another. I find myself occasionally wondering how the road might be different had other choices been selected, the experiences that might have been, the different people I might have found. It's hard to imagine beyond a fleeting moment. An alternate path would mean less of the one I'm on. I can't imagine anything I would give up, the good or the struggle.

In a short while, my Mesetas will end, give way to the greener rolling of another part of my journey. I'm excited for the road ahead, trying not to anticipate; melancholy time is passing so quickly. I hope I'm spending my days wisely, choosing the right path.

CONTRAST

I'm in Astorga; five hours lie between here and the end of the Mesetas. Then starts a climb over the Leónese Mountains; a full day's trek to get up one side and down the back.

Monday, I took a day off from my walking in León. After traveling two full weeks, some 425 kilometers /250 miles, my feet and knees were demanding it of me. A pleasant hotel in the historic district provided an alternative to refugio life. A classic European style, it offered a small elegant room with a full, deep bathtub—pure heaven for feet, knees, and my other body parts feeling the distance. Much of the Sunday after arriving was spent in a sidewalk café near the massive cathedral. There I took in a ritual of the Spanish, strolling through the old town area, something in which young and old, families and singles all seem to participate. Evenings between 6:00 and 8:00 p.m., before the late-ish dinner hour, the entire city is out seeing and being seen.

Monday noon refreshed, an assortment of tasks completed, I was back people watching when a realization set in. No one in the city had said hola, buenos días, Buen Camino to me. No one waved or acknowledged my presence. The people of the city are tending to their business, walking, talking on phones, chatting with companions. Those traveling solo remain face forward or to the ground. Eye contact is rare, a smile less so, an hola nonexistent. After being welcomed so overtly for two weeks, it was a stark contrast. In the biggest city, with hundreds of thousands of people, temporarily away from my fellowship of pilgrims, I began to feel isolated and anonymous among the crowd.

It was an uncomfortable shift.

It's not Spain, not León. Multi-tasking, busy, impersonal except with known friends, I found it harsh coming in from the plains where many know my name, ask about my home, inquire how I am doing. Seemingly everyone acknowledges my travel, my pilgrim adventure, in the small towns. In the cities there is no similar treatment. I've witnessed it before, experienced aloneness on business trips in major centers of America, Canada and other countries. It's the modern era, the style of the contemporary world.

Peregrinos are obvious in villages with small populations and then become a tiny minority in large cities. We see each other through the crowd, nod an acknowledgement across a distance—but are not part of the local life. I feel a kind of parallel universe around the Camino, where other rituals and routines apply. These bring a seemingly natural, open, emotional attitude from others and encourage something similar in me. It offers an easy connection to the fellow citizens of my parallel world. In the middle of Spain, though, in León, I stepped out of that pilgrim universe for a day, found it less than the ideal of my walking experience.

I lost my sense of peace.

The exception to what seemed a kind of invisibility I found in the old Spanish women and men. They see me from their benches along rivers and in town squares, in the pews of their churches. They see the signs of my walk, recognize dusty boots and sandals, zipper-legged cargo pants, the ginger steps of sore feet. Their eye contact acknowledges my journey. They believe in the purpose of pilgrimage, admire a willingness to try it on for size. I feel a special twinge when they smile at me. It's a knowing smile of wisdom tempered by a "been-there-done-that" life. I find it brings an emotional reaction for me. It's good.

Tuesday, after the day's rest, I returned to the country, setting out before dawn, taking ninety minutes to leave city sidewalks in favor of my dirt path. With sunrise came my first hola, then a Buen Camino. It was Pat, a South African woman I've been walking with on and off for a few days. She travels with a protracted limp, her gate obvious from a distance as I draw up from behind. The disconnected feelings of the previous day were gone a few hours later, check-in at the refugio in Hospital de Orbigo signaling my full return to the comfort of the pilgrim family.

I spent much of the day's trek wondering how much my home life mimics that of León, how many people I pass each day without looking their way. I felt a slight unease when I couldn't answer how often I smile at strangers.

THE CRUZ

The mountains of León lie to the east, along with the Mesetas. I've covered them both. I'm traveling the valley between the last two mountain ranges—Leónese behind, those ahead the Sierras. Today I walked passed the 200-kilometre, 120-mile marker. Villafranca is home tonight. Distance continues to dwindle.

    I crossed a significant point in the journey yesterday. It stands atop the Leónese Mountains. Known as the Cruz de Ferro (Iron Cross), it holds much anticipation for walkers. The Cruz, or cross, stands on a tall pole, three hours climb up the slope to the summit. Surrounding the cross and pole is a huge pile of rocks, each one placed there individually by a passing pilgrim. The tradition of the Cruz is to bring a small stone from home, carry it almost six hundred kilometers to the mountaintop, and leave it as a symbol of one's pilgrimage for others who come after. The weight of the accumulated stones and the travelers walking over them breaks the stones to small pieces and eventually to powder, the pile less rock than dust, making it even more significant than first appearance. The rocks represent many countries of the world, a kind of ad hoc United Nations work. Six years ago, Sandra and I left a stone, one from our home in the country. It now lies beneath a half million other stones—

the number of pilgrims who have walked since I was last here.

The tradition has broadened recently to include stones brought as symbols of intentions, these as varied as the people who carry them to the cross. Tina and Claire I met in Rabanal del Camino, a common overnight stop at the base of the mountain where I stayed before my uphill walk. Breast cancer survivors both, Claire's hair is shorter than mine—the indication of a recent battle with the disease. They belong to a world-class women's dragon boat team, the other members also cancer survivors. The two carry several stones between them, the purpose of each held private. Barry and Joe I also met in Rabanal. The two are another pairing from Ireland—Derrymen they were specific to point out. Barry's daughter experienced complications during childbirth five years ago, pain a constant companion for her since. Several operations have not relieved the difficulties. A dramatic recent attempt by doctors to repair the damage has her recuperating; the two men walk and pray during her hospital stay, hoping she'll be home before they return.

A Cruz tradition in Rabanal involves a blessing of the rocks the night before the trek to the top of the mountain. Tina, Claire, Barry, Joe, and I were gathered at the church for the blessing at 7:00 p.m. when it was discovered the three monks who perform the ceremony were away. Barry asked Joe to stand in and offer the blessing; with seven children to his credit, he seemed the most qualified. The five of us held hands, rocks in each connecting pair, while Joe offered beautiful words of prayer, hope, and inspiration. Intentions having just been shared among the group, emotions were hard to hold back. Barry excused himself immediately after Joe's words, worry for his daughter easily causing tears.

This has been a year of tribulation for me. The economy crashing was a blow, though it amounted to nothing a few months later when last November, Sandra's mother passed away, still quite young. Christmas brought the departure from my job of several years, a place I had been unhappy for some time. We knew the timing bad for me to leave between the economy and turning fifty-five, yet it was necessary. My mother's aging and another significant event added more change to the year, Michael's passing in June a major and traumatic blow.

There was a lot to think about when I decided to walk, the tradition of the Cruz coming to mind early. My question: How many rocks to bring and for what purpose?

I climbed the mountain with five stones in my backpack, the remainder of the ten brought onto the plane from home. The first five I left in Pamplona, parting with those I had parted with expectations I didn't wish to carry. Of the remaining five, one is from Sandra; the other four belong to me.

Mine represent attitudes and behaviors accumulated over years—some consciously, some unconsciously. They served a purpose once but, like old boxes in the attic, are no longer useful, occupy space, and block access to other valuables. After considering the year, inspired by the lives of Michael and Amira and taking the available time off for thought and change, the desire to let go of old boxes was what I brought to the mountain, to the cross. Attitudes and habits I no longer need or want. The economy, jobs, and other such things are necessary, will right themselves over time, but otherwise are insignificant. The relationships in my life, those I love, are of true value and purpose. I've always known this, but spending a few weeks away reminds me intimately that I need to pay attention to every day, cherish always each moment. It's too easy to be casual about time. The rocks symbolize my desire for change.

Starting out early, I arrived at the Cruz de Ferro just after sunrise. A dozen other pilgrim travelers already present, a few stood on the pile placing stones, others chatted at the bottom, some deep in personal thought. Waiting until others had come down, I climbed the rock pile to the centre, reaching the pole supporting the cross. From there I tossed each of my five stones, one by one, a few feet away—Sandra's first, then my four—each in a different direction. Collectively, our five stones formed a circle a few feet from the cross at the top of the pile, the one containing our earlier stone. The six symbolize love and promise.

I was pleased with the choice I made, the things I brought to the mountains of León. I felt it as I stood there, atop the pile next to the Cruz, hand empty of stones.

I walked west a few minutes later, sun rising behind the cross. I felt both shine on my back as I moved away.

My pack is now lighter, and my heart is too. I can sense the smile within.

TWO DAYS

I'm still here but was in small villages with limited or no access to Internet for the last few days. It was probably for the best, as the tone of this blog would have been frustration—my mood for most of Saturday and Sunday.

Saturday saw a long walk through the dramatic Valcarce Valley, a deep V-cut between two five hundred-foot sides, the valley floor a meandering creek and equally twisting two-lane blacktop. A path between the two is a safe and beautiful walking space for pilgrims. The path, road, and waterway consume the width of the valley floor, sun only capable of peeking over the rim by late morning. The valley ends some six hours walk from Villafranca where I started, the way out at the end a steep two thousand-foot hike up the Sierras to the eleventh-century mountaintop village of O'Cebreiro. The climb adds two to three hours of hard travel at the end of a long day. O'Cebreiro, though, is known by many as one of the most idyllic towns of the Camino, slate-topped stone houses, matching pedestrian only streets, fairytale imagery the reward for sweat spent to reach the summit.

The sun didn't show on Saturday. Overcast, cool weather came with the day, as it has for several now. Nearing the end of the valley, rain joined my walk for the climb ahead. It was the only company I found for my traveling hours. A brief respite from cloud cover near the top allowed a few pictures of the valley behind and then enclosed the mountain again. Heavy rain and dense fog demanded I remain indoors for the afternoon and evening as it did all others in the summit-top village, locales, tourists, and pilgrims alike. The weather resulted in a crowded refugio, cafés, and restaurants; I found it overpowering after the quiet and sparsely populated previous evenings. It was hard to shut out the noise; there seemed no place to hide from it.

    Sunday morning saw the fog lift, but overcast skies continued the on and off rain. A cool wind followed my steps along the alto ridge, hard at times to keep properly warm. The absence of familiar faces continued, those I assume had stopped in different towns perhaps decided to climb to O'Cebreiro when fresher on the Sunday morning. I spent hours alone both days, grey skies asking why I walked. I had the same question. Mid-afternoon I rounded a side hill twenty minutes from Samos, my intended home for Sunday night. The magnificent sixteenth-century Benedictine Monastery of Samos seemed to fill the entire valley below at that moment, a massive grey stone structure surrounded by rolling green hills. The scene lifted me a little; it's quite breathtaking. The Camino refugio along one side of the monastery were the last steps I needed in the still threatening weather. A hot shower, clean clothes, and good food helped ease my out-of-sorts disposition. But it was the evening events that brought me fully back.

The monastery has a spectacular chapel within and on its own would be a significant cathedral. Designed in the traditional Latin-cross style, ten-by-ten-foot-square columns along each side reach upward to a barrel-vaulted ceiling some six stories above. At the intersection of the crossbar, a dome crowns the church, it opening upward another few stories beyond the barrel vault with grand effect. Directly beneath the dome is the altar, last night adorned with varieties of many white flowers and much greenery. A flying cross is positioned a few feet above the surface of the table, near invisible wires creating the impression of its suspension in midair. I found it extraordinary to sit in the quiet and warmth of the church; the hard edge of the day seemed to crack. Vespers began at 7:15, chanting monks in the old building an instantly powerful sense of the spiritual and the sacred. The longer I sat, the more my spirit softened, Camino returned. The monks added incense midway through their prayers, smoke spiraling upwards to the dome, the chain and censer clanging a reverent ambience. The scent filled the chapel for all, but I thought somehow the fragrance and ritual were for me alone. More softening. The jagged feelings of two days seemed to rise and disappear with the incense, my inner space replaced with the familiar gentleness I've come to know over the past weeks.

Monday, offbeat weather continued, but the calm and peacefulness of the night before remained, maintained my inner balance for the day. I arrived in Portomarin to breaking clouds and a small, out-of-the-way private albergue. Two other albergues had been full, but the owner of the latter one had personally taken me across town to Manuel's. New beds, private bathrooms, and a proprietor who offered to wash and dry my clothes for a few dollars was heaven sent. Two days of rain had made it difficult to clean clothes, harder still to dry them properly.

The Spanish woman at Manuel's Albergue was an angel of mercy.

Santiago de Compostela lies ninety kilometers from here, about fifty-five miles to the west. Four hundred miles of Camino trail lie to the east; over 650 kilometers have been covered in 22 days. The last mountain range is behind me; rolling countryside and quiet forest is anticipated for much of the remaining days.

TWENTY-FIVE MILES

Azura is where I am tonight, forty kilometers, or about twenty-five miles, from the Cathedral of St. James in Santiago de Compostela. The unimaginable, initially eight hundred kilometers I faced four weeks ago, is in the past. Unimaginable now is that barely a day's travel remains after such a great distance. I can walk it all tomorrow, twenty-five miles near the outer edge of my capacity. I'd arrive tired if I did, likely enjoying the last hours of my last day less than I want. There is, however, another reason to spend two days rather than one to complete the remaining distance.

Lavacolla sits thirty kilometers from Azura, about two and a half hours walk from the cathedral and my final destination. It is renowned for a small stream where pilgrim walkers traditionally wash before entering Santiago, for some the event physical, for others it is an expectation of something spiritual. For these, the idea of a spiritual cleansing is a ritual undertaken before arrival at the church of St. James. The various traditions fall from ancient history when thirty days of walking required serious cleaning. I've decided to stop and follow the tradition. I'm not sure what to expect, so as has been the theme of my walk; I'll try to have no expectation. Hopefully there will be a bed to allow an overnight stay at the local albergue. The stop will leave a gentle distance remaining Friday morning, waiting until daylight to start, arriving in the historic district of Santiago late morning.

There is a saying that the Camino provides what an individual walker needs. The phrase applies to small events, like the woman who did my laundry the other evening after two days of rain left me without clean clothes, or a cold stream springing from beneath a church in the middle of the Mesetas—a medicinal remedy for sore feet. The expression also refers to experiences where it feels as though God has intervened: the man with the bucket of yellow paint or the taxi driver who directed me in the dark of morning when lost. A broader interpretation belongs to the entire pilgrimage walk, a sense the month-long experience touches something deep within. It has for me on both occasions.

My first walk connected me with people who had a significant impact, one a fellow from San Francisco whom I paced for most of the 2003 journey. He and I became very close during our travel, meeting off and on a number of evenings, as well as along the path during our days. Approximately my age, we shared the events of our respective lives, our successes and trials, families' stories, and personal experiences—some similar, some very different, but all moving. I treasured our conversations, was deeply disappointed we inadvertently parted on the last day without exchanging contact information. I walked with a Danish fellow for a few days at the end of my 2003 walk, the man a retired music professor. His was a beautiful soul, inspiring—something I attributed to his love of art, music, and literature. Again we shared a close connection that rarely occurs so quickly between men who have just met. One morning over coffee, he described a beautiful tradition we both faced when arriving at the Cathedral de Santiago. The passionate description brought tears to his eyes; the intimacy with which he spoke did the same for me. And there was Javier—the man whose appearance was of an ancient prophet—who spoke with such beauty, I felt as though he might be.

As much as I tried this year to arrive without expectations, I still anticipated connections to people who might touch and inspire me. I expected as much for a few hundred miles. It hasn't happened.

This walk has been mostly a solitary journey. The first week, Jill accompanied me for much of the time. Great company, she was akin to one of my siblings, equally easy with banter, intellect, humor, and personal conversation. The candidness of our conversations set what I hoped would be the tone for my time walking.

I have since met people with touching stories, but none similar to my previous experience. Since that first week, I have walked mostly alone. Perhaps this was what I needed more than inspiration—time to be alone. It feels as though it might be.

The time has been introspective, an opportunity to consider the year that's been, the loves of my life. I have been deeply blessed with relationships, the loss of two in eight months bringing a time to fully appreciate how blessed. Even the luxury of this walk, despite the manner in which it came to me, is something I need to fully appreciate. I've been given time to be present for myself and for others as the events of the year have unfolded. Perhaps the greater impact of Spain has been to spend time to appreciate this. As my walk comes to a close, I feel I've missed little, the time and effort spent to cross Spain the best thing I could have done.

But I've missed home. Since Pamplona, my first steps, I've been walking west in the direction of my home, of Sandra, my mother, and of my siblings in the US and Canada. In León, almost two weeks ago, the feeling of my walk changed. Since then, I've been pulled toward home, heart first. It has been a glorious, contemplative time to travel the ancient trail again, and I'm saddened to realize it's coming to a conclusion. The pull of home, though, is stronger. The Camino has provided what I needed—personal time. I've been able to talk to God and be in a place quiet enough to listen for his response. Some of the conversations found their way into my head and heart. I understand and feel this now. Much I believe will come in the weeks and months ahead. The calm and peacefulness within my soul I hope will remain a long, long time.

Walking into Santiago, I'm again trying not to anticipate; Friday morning will be unique to this experience. I have the weekend in Compostela, a further few days with my thoughts to understand more of my time, more of my feelings from the walk across Spain.

THIRTY-SIX HOURS

Lavacolla didn't work as a place to stay, but a tiny hamlet twenty minutes farther along did—a quiet semi-farming village of less than a hundred people. Partially awake Friday before a rooster sounded nearby, I packed and headed out. Christiane, a recently retired French woman who walked with me the day before also arose, joined in the silent trek of my last remaining hilltop before Santiago de Compostela. Sunrise broke before 8:00, its presence between the city buildings a couple of hours later visible only on rare occasion during the last of my walk in Spain. As 9:00 approached, feet still fresh and barely a light sweat breaking on my forehead, the old city appeared down the block, cathedral spires of the historic district visible a few hundred feet beyond where I stood. Less than a few minutes of the walk remained.

Obradoiro Square, a double-wide, football-sized field of grey cobblestone sits in front of the twin-towered facade of the Cathedral of Saint James. The last of my Camino took me to the centre of the square, standing in awe of the ornate church, the effort required to reach it swirling surreal in my head. Magnificent simply by itself, after twenty-six days and almost five hundred miles, the sight brought emotion near the surface. Christiane stood beside me, several other pilgrims nearby. The silence from each spoke of similar feelings. It was a long journey, unimaginable. Yet I stood in the square, about to enter the church, final footsteps of the walk less than a few meters away.

The pilgrims' mass is celebrated in the cathedral each day at 12:00. Beginning with one of the four celebrating priests reciting from a list, the nationality and starting point of each walker issued a Compostela is read aloud, each having received the certificate of completion at the Pilgrim's Office within the previous twenty-four hours. Hearing them call out that a Canadian, starting in Pamplona, had arrived that morning continued the emotion begun outside. The cathedral is truly massive, the inner sanctum having a seating capacity of almost a thousand. The wide U-shaped ambulatory, the crossbar sides, and other standing areas around the edges fill to overflowing; some 1,200–1,500 are in attendance for noon mass each day. Many in the crowd wear hiking boots and sandals, zipper-legged cargo pants and T-shirts, outward symbols of a journey completed that morning, perhaps a day or two earlier. Many faces in the crowd were familiar to me, from cities and towns east, more than a few with wet eyes. Somewhere along the thin line of dirt across the Iberian Peninsula we had become pilgrims, the many who stood inside the Cathedral de Santiago with me yesterday. Not sure where nor how it occurred, hearts told us—told me—of the transition. There was joyful richness within, uncontainable. Tears neared the surface as the reality of arrival settled.

Close to where I stood was Claude, a short-ish, middle-aged Frenchman, his dark wavy hair worn in a ponytail. Walking from the Alps in eastern France, his feet covered more than twice the distance I traveled. His girlfriend—the tall, beautiful, and blonde Christine—accompanied him in the cathedral. I first met Claude walking by himself three weeks earlier, crossing a substantial plateau. Having already covered a thousand kilometers, his pace was faster, sweeping up quickly from behind me. Slowing along side, he nodded, and we fell into easy conversation for a short while. His voice soft and debonair, Claude struck me as elegant, bearing a demeanor gentle and genuine. We spoke briefly of our respective homes, our journey thus far, of where we headed for the night. A short while later, he resumed the faster pace, waving farewell as he moved ahead. A few moments later, barely a dozen paces from me, Claude turned to look over his shoulder. "The peace of God be with you," he called back. "I will pray for you as I walk." I was deeply touched by his words, the gesture somehow felt profound, as we had been strangers just minutes earlier. Perhaps it was the sincerity I sensed in his voice, but I felt certain I would be in the man's prayers. The image he cast, Claude's words, and the sound of his voice remained long after the Frenchman disappeared over the horizon. I encountered Claude again on several occasions—sometimes with Christine; other times alone. The encounter was always brief; each occasion I received the same beautiful, welcoming smile.

In the cathedral, Claude stood next to Christine, the two holding hands, unaware I had arrived behind them. I tapped a shoulder gently. When Claude turned, his eyes lit up, and dropping Christine's hand, I was hugged tightly, the soft voice in my ear. "I have thought of you often, kept you in my prayers. You have been with me on my walk, and you will be with me after I return home." Stepping back from our embrace, the Frenchman put his hand to his heart, spoke gently again, "You are my brother." We stared into each other's eyes for long moments.

I felt deeply touched by the man from the Alps and don't really understand why Claude's impact on me was so great. I found it extraordinary to be treated so beautifully by someone I would otherwise consider a stranger. Yet something connected the two of us, something of the path we both shared, for I felt the same toward the man from France. We were far from strangers; we are fellow pilgrims. His words I echoed back in my heart, fumbled something less eloquent out loud.

I stood with Claude and Christine for the mass, next to me Christiane, who shared the last days of my walk, and Jill, the English therapist from my first week. Jill had made it into Santiago a day earlier, was looking for me at the pilgrims' mass. As she arrived to stand with us, I understood immediately she too had an enormous impact on my walk. I felt again Jill seemed a sister in those moments when we hugged, our personal time together grown in meaning since we had parted. I thought often of Jill in the weeks since Burgos, had worried we might not reconnect in Santiago before returning to our homes.

We stood in the cathedral, the little group that became my personal family of pilgrims: Jill, Claude, and Christiane. Jill I walked with seven days at the outset, Christiane the last three, Claude but a few hours in between. Each was as close to my heart as the next. Much of my time walking the Camino was solitary, but there had indeed been special people. I hadn't understood it fully until Santiago. I stood with them all for the pilgrims' mass in the Cathedral of St. James. The ceremony ended, though our tiny collection of pilgrims remained, the others being introduced to one another as we chatted. Claude spoke of sadness brought on by the end of his walk, lifted by high emotion at the Pilgrim's Mass. It brought closure to his walk, the mass had; a true celebration of what he had accomplished. My heart felt the same; we each nodded agreement with the words. Christiane offered the mass was beautiful wrapping of the inner present that was our individual Caminos. More agreement. The fingerprints of God I sensed all over the present. The church remained crowded long after mass concluded, groups such as ours sharing laughter, tears, and introductions as much, I assumed, as we did.

The gathering seemed to crown several beautiful, touching events that began thirty-six hours earlier.

My father died in 1997. His passing left a large hole in my heart filled by a lifetime of great memories and the love and faith he and my mother offered unconditionally. One of my sisters, Tishie, speaks of sitting at her cottage one evening, talking to my father after his passing. Asking for a sign he was with her in the solitary moment, a shooting star lit the night sky as she finished the thought. Patricia told me of the event recently, saying she now thinks of shooting stars with my father. She has seen them on numerous occasions. I love her connection between the two and have remembered it since I first heard the story. Leaving Azura, the fog of the previous mornings absent, a brilliant starry sky followed me out to the country. Ten minutes from the lights of town, buildings faded behind, the sky was more obvious without the glow of civilization. On Thursday morning, the last full day of my walk across Spain, a few minutes out of Azura, a shooting star lit the predawn sky. I don't know why I looked up; the darkened trail a more important focus to keep from stumbling. The star's trail seemed to start over the town I had just left and flew perfectly west—the direction of Santiago de Compostela. I stopped for a moment, my sister's connection in my heart. My father was pointing the way home to Santiago, I decided. It is a beautiful moment. I will treasure it long after I've left this country.

Christiane I met walking into Azura the day before the shooting star, a few hours before arriving at the overnight stop in Azura. It became apparent shortly after we connected the French woman has both a beautiful inner spirit and a deep sense of the spiritual. Our conversations moved easily to the spirituality the walk created for each of us, the transition occurring from long days of both natural beauty and physical exertion. That evening, sitting together, Christiane explained her husband had walked the Camino several years earlier, meeting a couple of companions his first day, traveling the entire country with the two others. Arriving at the stream near Lavacolla, where ceremonial bathing occurs, the three washed each other's feet as part of their journey.

I listened intently as Christiane described the event, her passion flowing for the great humility this event represented to her. My fellow pilgrim then surprised me with a question, asked if she could wash my feet at the stream if we still walked together when it arrived. I was taken aback by both the question and my reaction to it; I was resistant to something that seemed so personal, humbled by her desire to show such vulnerability to someone just met.

Twenty-four hours later, the evening before walking into Santiago, we were together by the stream near the tiny hamlet just beyond Lavacolla, Christiane bent over with towel in hand, while I sat on a flat-topped rock. It was then Christiane washed my feet. Drying them a moment later, she asked how I felt. *Humbled* was the only word I could get out. She stood, declaring she felt the same. The gift of humility, she then called it. We changed places so I could reciprocate, wash Christiane's feet. It was in that moment I remembered my night at the refugio in Tosantos.

Juan Jose, my host that night during our meditation in the upper room three weeks earlier, had recited from a small book the definition of a pilgrim: humble and simple of life, accepting everything received gratefully. The words had remained with me the entire journey, returning often. Simple and grateful I decided I could be, was doing so on my walk. Humility, though, seemed not as easy to evaluate. I found myself asking the definition of humility. Who decides the measurement or when it's been met? I found the answer to my question at the stream ten kilometers from Santiago de Compostela. Humility, for me, is now clearly defined by the experience of washing feet. I truly felt it, as someone I recently met had the personal strength, courage, and humility to wash my feet, asking me to gratefully accept it as a gift, the manner in which it was offered. Humility was the only means by which I felt the kindness could be offered, the only way it could be received. I was touched deep inside by the moment.

The shooting star, a profound and personal ceremony of feet washing, the pilgrims' mass, Christiane, and the reconnection with Jill and Claude—these were deeply felt, perhaps a closing bookend of a sort, the last day and a half of my pilgrimage walk across Spain.

The Camino provides what the pilgrims need I've been told. I would add it seems to come only when I needed it, and I was ready to accept gratefully. I walked much of my journey alone. I now understand I needed the time to be alone. When I needed others, they were there—some casually, three profoundly. The events of my last thirty-six hours added a crown of beautiful emotion and inner clarity to my nearly four weeks of walking. The events and memory of the emotion will remain with me always.

Expectation followed my entire journey. I tried to rid myself of the feeling, but it came along for the walk anyway. The Camino, the fingerprints of God, seemed more than capable of working around them, didn't allow expectation to inhibit the beauty of the people I met along the way to Santiago. Three in particular—Jill, Claude, and Christiane—I knew for a brief time, am unlikely to see ever again after I leave Spain. Yet the inner spirit and spirituality of each inspired me greatly. They were all touched by the presence of God and the peculiar experience of pilgrimage, as am I. We experienced something unique to each of us, shared the transition to pilgrims as something common to all. These three, and my other experiences, forever leave fingerprints on my heart.

THE LOOKING GLASS

The historic district of Santiago de Compostela is the image of old world Europe; ancient buildings crowd shoulder to shoulder, colors of sand and gold and hues of brown and grays, roofs of tile and slate, impossibly crooked and narrow paving-stone inlaid streets, all of hap hazard arrangement. A great cathedral and huge cobblestone square anchor all from the centre. Along every street and passageway, tables and chairs litter the sides; it is impossible to know which set belongs to which cafe. I feel at home in the twisting confines.

The beauty of the old city is a lovely draw but not the primary one for me. Having spent almost a month walking Spain, the streets and cafes hold another treasure; the faces of peregrinos I've met. Jill, Claude, Christine, Christiane, Marcus, Lillianne, Suzanne, Julliet, Enrico—these and other names are pilgrims I met. Still others are faces I recognize for which I don't have names. Some, like Jill, arrived before me, others a day or two later. I meet them in the cathedral, stumble upon one or more in shops, and am called to by a group under a sun umbrella at a cafe. Fellow pilgrims are the fabric of the welcome I feel in Santiago de Compostela. The chance encounters with fellow walkers migrate to a lunch, a chat over espresso, a stop for wine, and stories of the road.

The faces are changed since we last were together. Mine too. In Burgos, León, and other places, we shared dinners, nearby bunk beds, or perhaps a part of the trail. No matter the circumstance, the road ahead was then unfinished—distance remained to be covered, our task not complete. Walking into Santiago the trek is done, completion invoking the change of facial expression we wear, though not simply as the miles of the Camino now lay behind. I walked a long way, strained and sweated outside, on occasion struggled inside. At times muscles hurt; the days earlier on were accompanied by fatigue and soreness. A few times, I didn't understand why I had come to Spain, felt alone—even lonely. As the days passed, Santiago drew closer, and I became physically stronger for continuing the effort. Emotions and the spiritual seemed at times to travel separate directions within me, though they too continued a path leading onward. And they too became stronger, richer, as the Camino unfolded. Last Friday, I was quietly euphoric as the final kilometers to the city in northwestern Spain passed underfoot, the walk—my walk—within an hour of completion, of accomplishment.

I did something very, very good for myself. It showed in my face as I entered the city. I could feel it in my eyes, my smile.

This sense of accomplishment, of having done something of greater inner purpose, I see on the face of other pilgrims, feel it as they stand near, hear it in their voice. These others can see, feel, and hear it in me. The experience is one of uncommon and beautiful kinship, of something deeply personal. Those I met and walked with, no matter how briefly, share this sense, became intimately connected by it. Claude said it best: we are brothers and sisters in the truest sense of the word. My walk of the Camino de Santiago offered a vividly felt experience, became a reminder of the connectedness of my inner spirit with the spirit of others. The inner journey for each pilgrim is as unique as our individual faces, the larger experience of pilgrimage something we share with each other. I shared it with all I met and know that as surely as I know my name. Others do as well. Somewhere in this lies the reason I meet others with great hugs in Santiago, emotion often near or flowing for both peregrinos. It's a common sight, repeated often in the streets of the old city. A casual congratulation or handshake is not enough to celebrate what happened. Hearts are in too grand a state, too full, a sense of the spiritual too present. Pilgrims don't seem to question whether a hug is appropriate; rather we fall into the arms of one another without hesitation.

As the day or two in Santiago unfolded, sadness nibbled the edges of my stay, the time to return home drawing close for me and for all. The walk I know in my heart is truly complete, the time to return to my other world near. I said farewell to Jill before she boarded a train bound for England. Somewhere during the Saturday, Claude and Christine also departed, the two of them for the return trip to France. That evening, Christiane's husband Alain arrived, the two planning time in Portugal to reconnect after time apart. We three celebrated the pilgrims' mass again Sunday noon and lingered over a long lunch through the afternoon; a drink later in the day the last time we said good-bye. The bond I developed with Christiane extended to Alain, fuelled in part by his own experience of a Camino walk of a few years earlier.

The Camino de Santiago became for me, a looking-glass experience. Not of tea parties and rabbits, this one filtered my life—the truly important from the merely necessary. For a month in the world of the Camino, the modern of my world was virtually and blissfully absent, a delicious personal time suspending the busyness of life, the noise of multitasking silent. I reconnected with inner peacefulness on the path across Spain. For me, and perhaps for those I met, the simplistic lifestyle and walk allowed my physical, emotional, and spiritual selves to become reacquainted, or perhaps rebalanced is the right term. The politeness, kindness, courtesy, consideration, and generosity of both walkers and villagers inspire on a grand scale. In the gentleness of the natural, the historic and the calm, my inner being, the inner being of other pilgrims, and the spirit of the divine intertwined to create a sense of harmony, perhaps even grace. Drawn in were the loves and blessings of my life, past and current, all wonderfully present as I walked. Left outside the looking glass were the nonessentials of my contemporary world.

I stepped into the looking glass of the Camino de Santiago four weeks ago at the end of August when I checked into the refugio in Pamplona. Monday morning, departing the pensión, where I stayed in Santiago, I carried my backpack across the old city one last time. At the modern commercial district on the perimeter, I located a taxi and, climbing in the back, was transported back through the looking glass. A few days earlier, it had taken over three hours to walk to the historic area of the city from Santiago airport. The taxi ride back took less than twenty minutes.

The difference felt surreal.

I stopped walking in Santiago de Compostela, but my pilgrimage journey didn't end there. Nor did I leave anything valuable behind as the taxi took me away from the old city. The personal, the intimate, and the spiritual came with me, back through the looking glass. I have come to think of my life as pilgrimage, the Camino de Santiago an opportunity by which I experience an encapsulated version—the innermost of my humanness in its purest form. I find the experience of God, of humanity, and of nature more alive, vibrant, and present while I walk, perhaps in the quiet, the slowness, and the calm; I feel them more fully. I take home in my heart the experiences of an amazing four weeks every minute of my walk. The travel was enough to deeply feel the emotion, the experience of everything and everyone I encountered, the resulting richness of heart I expect to linger a long time. I also have on my soul the fingerprints of God; these I felt through the places, events, and people I encountered—each reaching inside, sometimes unknown by me, and touched deeply, reached my soul. The imprints are there forever, added to others I've accumulated elsewhere along the journey, the pilgrimage of life.

My prayer as I return is to have greater trust and awareness of the yellow arrows in my life, of divine intervention. Walking tomorrow along my path, I believe painters of yellow arrows go before me. Sometimes the posted guide marker is only splashed up the moment I arrive. It is easy to fall into old habits, the busyness of life again, and miss an arrow that might direct me to another path. This I expect is the hardest to avoid.

I want to be present to myself and those I love one day at a time, let go the past, travel slow enough to feel the journey fully, keep my eyes toward the faces of others. And be conscious for the possibility of yellow arrows.

Humility, simplicity, and gratefulness I need to develop more as my cornerstones.

Buen Camino.

Me, On the Road to Santiago in 2009

Pamplona City Hall

Monastery Refugio at Samos

My Celtic Cottage Refugio

Amigo de Peregrino, Painting Yellow Arrows

Placing Stones at the Cruz de Ferro

Washing Feet Near Lavacolla

Mikie & The Cathedral of St. James, Santiago de Compostela

Epilogue–Part I

2009 is relegated to the pages of history, and with it my second pilgrimage has been embedded in my DNA. Unlike other vacations and trips abroad, the details of my month in Spain are as crisp now as the day I experienced them, and even 2003 is still a very clear picture within. And though the two walks were quite different and unique from one another, the emotional and spiritual high of pilgrimage was common to both.

The slowness of walking across a country allowed my eyes to fully focus and properly imprint the beauty of what I saw; my heart and soul were so unhurried by distractions as to genuinely feel the experiences of time alone with just me. One thing is certain; the loveliness lingers within. I hope I have not seen the last of the Camino de Santiago, though it's hard to image how I might find myself there again.

"I'm not here to learn, I'm here to feel."

The words Javier had spoken during one of the first days of my first walk have indeed been prophetic.

Learning happens for me no matter what, but the essence I took from Javier's words was about how information and experiences are filtered; head first, or heart first. All is accumulated as part of who I am, but the two filters of head and heart can have a dramatically different effect on what I learn, and the lessons I take away. The Camino was first and foremost about experiences of the heart. I did learn along the way, but the learning was brought to me through the emotional, and less through intellect.

The difference was and is profound.

I now believe that prior to 2003, my faith journey was more heavily oriented to an intellectual understanding than it was to spiritual relationship. Both are components of the overall nature of a faith journey, but I think for me the balance was off prior to pilgrimage entering my world. There was too much head and not enough heart. So my first 500 mile walk did educate me in a way; it taught me about the yin and yang of this balance, so to speak, and of how to realign the two so as to have the right amount of each. I came away from Santiago the first time with a better perspective of this. Some of the rebalancing was lost to time in the years following 2003, but much remained. A good portion was firmly embedded within my soul.

My second walk brought experiences to again remind me of the role these two ingredients play, and about their influence on my daily life, and life's journey through time. For me, their balance is key in my journey towards God, and to recognize the truly important parts of my life which guide me on the road I travel.

Pilgrimage was spiritually and emotionally extraordinary, or at least it was from my experience of the one running across the Iberian Peninsula. As unusual and perhaps odd as the Camino de Santiago seemed before walking the first time, it was neither during my time in Spain nor after the walks ended. Gentle and of great peace, my best summation is that it offered beautiful parallels to my other world, the one I've resumed now that I'm home. It did so as a kind of microcosm of the ideal, in the sense it highlighted the truly important and valuable of my life's journey, and re-focused my emotional and spiritual energy. The simplicity and quiet of a month trekking an ancient footpath, away from the stress of the multitasking and at times confounding world offered time to both live pilgrimage, and reflect on its purpose for me. From citizen of the contemporary to some kind of pilgrim visiting the past, I came away from the meditative, transformative journey with much gain and surprisingly, some loss.

I travel a winding road across the years of my life, the long pilgrimage journey from birth to the hereafter. Through the decades, with encounters simple and extravagant, accented by beauty and struggle, I've come to accept I'm being led toward something sacred. Whether I call this God, which I do, or something else seems less important than that I acknowledge my journey as a move toward the Divine. Somewhere mixed in with this, I believe is the purpose of my life, or at least steps that lead to a greater understanding of it. Both pilgrimage walks of the Camino gave me an opportunity to appreciate this more fully, doing so by separating me from contemporary entanglements long enough to gain a deep experience of the spiritual. The trek of the Camino de Santiago offered me a perspective of life's journey through a different lens; one that allowed me to sense God more personally.

The first third of my Camino was, without conscious awareness of it at the time, heavily oriented on the physical; where I was going, how I'd get there, how hard it would be. I asked often whether my body would be as strong and as capable as I needed it to be.

Satisfying myself that failing accident or injury I was going to make the distance, I shifted as the second part of the walk commenced. The walk across the arid flat land of central Spain encouraged an unconscious transition to a more introspective time; I undertook a personal assessment, 'taking stock' of my emotional and spiritual being. The transition from physical to emotional and spiritual is subtle, seemingly as natural a progression as was the continuing trail passing underfoot. It was not dissimilar to my life. As I moved beyond my early adult years, so too my life became less focused on the physical and shifted to be more internally concerned; I strived to develop a well rounded, balanced self in the context of the emotional and spiritual surroundings I found myself. I succeeded partially, though emotional and spiritual shaping I conclude is a lifelong exercise; there is no final destination.

With this I am a work in progress, with much still to be done.

The third leg of my walk across Spain carried me toward the deeper 'capital S' of Spiritual consideration and discovery, something I found happens for many who travel the ancient road, experiencing with it the great peace of pilgrimage. Each day I walked brought greater awareness of God's presence and in turn I became open to an instinctual guidance that seemed provided to me. I became attentive to the details of people and situations which I had previously ignored or assigned as co-incidence. I found myself alert to how the encounters made me feel, whether they touched me in some unusual manner. I felt I became more spiritually aware, something the busyness of life at home often curtails. With time, tranquility and an awareness of the Spiritual on the Camino, I found I could discern greater intimacy from my experiences. Some things were indeed coincidence; others, clearly for me at least, were not. Having learned from many encounters large and small along the Iberian trail, I developed a trust that saw me eventually hand my care fully over to the Divine.

I hoped to bring this attitude back from Spain with me; though in truth I still struggle to find a way to live it daily.

On the Camino I moved beyond the premise that events are always co-incidence or synchronistic, to a full acceptance that some encounters uniquely found me, came to my path, and had a purpose beyond the simplistic. Some experiences were a moment of pure joy, some profound enough to move my heart greatly and touch me deep inside; some experiences had value for my soul. I stopped seeing these as good and bad, beauty and struggle, greater or less so. Each came and went, each with a kind of unique spiritual aura to it. My task was simply to accept and appreciate the circumstance, for however long, as each event unfolded. Some experiences led me to another stepping stone, connecting me with my path. Some were but a moment in time and then gone. In the world of my daily life, these types of events are rarely something I take time to fully appreciate. I can easily be oblivious to them, or even judgmental about their seeming interference with my schedule; it is a constant struggle for me to constrain both these attitudes. In Spain I slowed sufficiently to recognize events going on all around me. I set aside any ability to pretend they were not there, or were of co-incidence.

Walking a pilgrimage I was cognizant of being fully in the present, the result to see and feel the richness and the moments of my surroundings.

Even more than one day at a time, my journey sometimes required a one-step-at-a-time attitude, another life similarity. The farther I traveled in Spain, the more frequently I seemed to come across situations where I needed to trust I would be looked after in a given circumstance; that there would be a bed for the night; that restaurants would be found in the next town; that I would find a bank machine to replenish dwindling cash reserves. On my first Camino, I elected to travel without maps or guide books, instead simply following the yellow arrows. With such an approach, detailed information was often scarce. In each situation I moved forward trusting when conventional experience might have dictated backtracking. In each circumstance, I found the answer was different than my expectations, but always meeting my true need instead of my perceived desires. I found a bed but also met interesting people with whom I walked. I found food, but the added experience of a family-style meal reminded me of growing up long ago. And I didn't find a cash machine for two days after the time I was certain I would need it. But twenty dollars stretched comfortably over several days, including meals, snacks and accommodations at half the usual price, allowing me to travel twice as far until I was able to locate the next bank machine. Interestingly, I wanted for nothing, and learned much about the generosity of circumstance and the potential of God's gentle hand. These experiences and others taught me more than the take-it-one-step-at-a-time; they taught me to trust in the outcome when I've handed things over to God's care.

Meeting people whose joys and struggles emulate my life has always been a high for me. In this I found a camaraderie born of pilgrimage experience which is somehow shared by most, perhaps even all who trek across Spain. It was heart warming to spend time traveling with these others, given the candidness and trust of strangers. Sharing intimate details of one's life in such an unprotected and easy style is truly uplifting. I have found this the foundation of true friendship in my life, and perhaps another reason why genuine relationships form easily in Spain. At home, and with age, this process of friendship has become harder to replicate. I haven't maintained reg-

brought a freeing attitude. With 99% of my possessions absent, I was surprised to find I lacked for nothing; my wants and needs were met physically, emotionally and spiritually each day as I journeyed. At home now, I try to entrench this understanding elsewhere in my life. I enjoy a middle class world, and don't see myself giving it up anytime soon. But I have simplified much over the last few years, and no longer have a desire for a bigger house, fancier car or the latest fashions. I do still like such things, but they're less important, less sought after now. And I still have my vices, travel predominant among them as the costliest. But even this I covet less.

I was reminded with possessions slimmed to absolute basics, it is humanness and individuality which reveal both my sameness with others, and my uniqueness from them. I found great beauty in the experience.

I realize through this writing I've retained some of the benefits of this philosophy, gained over two walks six years apart. In Spain, I learned to accept each day as a pilgrim, sharing the transitional experience with other pilgrims. I spent a month living richly if not rich, genuinely comfortable with only the essentials, and participating fully in the moment, worrying not about either past or future.

An outgrowth of the experience has been to push back against too much technology in my life; I've begun controlling its presence in my world. I enjoyed the absence of mobile phone and computer on my walk. I've long known of their value and necessity, but realized through their absence on my walk just how distractive is their nature. I'm not naive enough to think of fully parting company with all my gadgets, but I am evaluating each new and upgraded technology before I allow it to become entrenched as part of my world. I've already simplified over the last decade, and I expect that process to continue. For this I'm truly grateful as my life now seems less cluttered and busy. Yet there has been a cost to this change. I am losing some connection to the contemporary world as a result of my decision. I feel at times 'left out,' when talk in my social circles moves to the detail of the latest and greatest new device. And certainly there are other personal and professional benefits I forego with this new tack.

I'm striving to find a balance between technology that supports and simplifies my life, and that which consumes time and energy I no longer wish to surrender to it.

I found the concept of the yellow arrows has a parallel to home life as well. On my original trip, I expected to travel Spain with the aid of maps and guides. But before setting out, I abandoned most of them to follow the painted arrows left by others that mark the way. The arrows can be depended upon to show the correct path, but curiously seemed to interact with instinct to create options about where to go and where to stay. My only way to describe this is to suggest it's a connectedness between my inner voice and something in the larger world around me. This discovery I must confess was totally unexpected. Following the painted arrows, occasionally asking others for direction, and at times being led by instinct brought curious and beautiful encounters I might have missed had I not given over to this process.

Fingerprints of God?

I certainly felt such occasions were inspired by something greater than just my imagination or co-incidence. I recall in each such instance, my heart encountering an intimate feeling of something naturally elegant. I might have simply walked by had it not been for a sense of following my heart. I'm trying to maintain this attitude at home, this pattern of letting instinct lead at times, and hope God is showing the way. It is an attitude intertwined with trust. I believe my greatest gain from pilgrimage is centered on this; a spiritual trust developed through my experiences of Spain.

My appreciation of God's ways has moved in a more personal direction, and my trust, real trust of this faith journey, has grown as a result.

Epilogue–Part II

The religious nature of my life's journey, the discipline and structure through which I have historically learned of Spirituality, has been changed somewhat by pilgrimage. This change comes not from failings of my church, perceived or real. The change comes from the complexity of religious dialogue in the contemporary world. Spirituality I experienced on my walk as elegantly simplistic, pure, and extravagantly loving. It is as natural and intrinsic as it is profound and personal. Even these words don't suffice, but I feel they reach in the best direction I can describe. The experience of pilgrimage touched my heart in a very real manner, and then went beyond to massage my soul. It was unquestionably about a genuine time in my relationship with God. Conflicts between science and religion, about the right and wrong of what is truth, seem disconnected from this personal experience.

My beliefs can feel complicated by the constant fight of science, human evolution, moral theology and church teaching. The battle seemingly has neither end, nor solution or harmony. I am one of those who can appreciate points raised by both sides in any of the well known arguments. Empathy has never been a failing of mine. Having been raised with church teachings, I know the case for the religious, and am comfortable they are based on truth. Living the contemporary world of science and technology, I understand the reliability of experiment and evidence. And having met people whose heart is in the right place but walk their own path seeking to resolve some personal conflict between the two, I can appreciate the road on which they travel. I have difficulty with such balance myself at times, finding solid ground between compassion and empathy for this reality on one side, and my desire to espouse what I believe on the other. Seeking spiritual reconciliation for my own weaknesses and spiritual brokenness is where I come out, not feeling adequate to question the decisions others make when I reflect properly on the circumstance.

This may render me less devout than some, but in reality I feel I live along a spectrum between conviction and confusion; it feels like forward motion measured over a life time, but involves many backwards steps along the way.

The gentleness, beauty and simplicity of God's style, as I experienced it from my pilgrimage journeys, are where I place my weight. In conjunction with this, I've migrated over time to rely on a particular biblical passage. At one point, Jesus is asked which commandment is the most important. He responds saying to love God, love neighbor and love self, and then goes on to say the rest of the law rests on these words. I believe if I truly love in such capacity, confusion and complexity drop away. My experience of Spirituality on the Camino aligns closely with this biblical teaching. The encounters of genuine and heartfelt people I came across, both travelers and those who host them, were experiences of love. My sense of their motivation was the capital S Spirituality, allowed to exist openly through the mystic of Camino ancestry. God is experienced there more fully perhaps for no greater reason than it is there people are willing to consider him fully. A month long walk brings close encounters with God because it is there love resides as he originally defined it.

I haven't abandoned my religious pursuit, but I have come to appreciate a primary obligation outside it is to identify my personal road to Spirituality. I must find my own unique and intimate relationship with God. It seems obvious, and perhaps should have been long ago. I would have no less expectation of any other relationship. I don't quite understand why I've treated this one so differently, but perhaps that is the journey everyone faces.

It certainly is mine.

Spending a month with God, in a place he clearly cares about, the Camino offered a better view of this kind of relationship. I had a great walk with him. In Spain, I found myself invoking prayer more often than I do at home; prayer and meditation. The practice of both I attribute to the environment of the Way of St. James; quiet, tranquil, contemplative, with the luxury of personal time devoid of high pressure, and the demands and distractions of contemporary life. There was time for prayer, and the natural surroundings produced the supporting meditative state. Both I'm told, are a means of connecting with God. I found on my trek across Spain I also combined prayer with casual conversation. With the beauty of so much time alone, embraced by the emotion of endless sky, open country, rich forests and mountain passes, it was easy to go deep inside. I shared my thoughts with God, and I had an extraordinary feeling he spoke back to me. Not with words, but with instinctual feelings, suggestions of the heart, that inner voice that seemed at times to dictate the directions of my feet and the encounters with people they took me to. My Spiritual relationship became more familial than it has ever been, one of the highest highs of a lifelong effort to understand and live a faith journey

I doubt that what I experienced on my walks of the Camino de Santiago would classify as miracles. I don't call them that, nor think of them as such. But my sense of the presence of God was unmistakable. Many events were simply too extraordinary to be anything less. I have experienced dryness of spirit in my life - the proverbial dark night of the soul; I am unfortunately familiar with it. And I have experienced the intimate high of knowing with certainty God is nearby, that I am somehow in his presence. I felt it during the last days of my father's life, and again during the last days with Michael, my brother-in-law. The hallmark of God's presence is the presence of pure, unselfish love. I felt this powerfully during my Camino walks, though without the pain of these other examples. I have felt it at many other times in my life, during both joy and struggle, on occasions where love is at its fullest. I can still, at times, forget the depth of exposure I've had to the Spiritual through these love encounters. But the center of my humanness, and experiences such as those of the Camino, keep me believing love as described in that biblical passage is the journey toward the Divine.

In Spain I believe I became more accountable to God and myself for my side of our relationship. The guidance of religious teachings, which influenced much thought and action along the road of my faith journey, are now subservient to this relationship. I may have once had it the other way around, at least in some respects. I accept the theological premise that God in his omnipotence is in many ways unknowable, and part of my journey requires understanding gained from a theological organization. Yet my sense is God makes himself knowable through truly loving encounters. It has taken a long time for me to fully appreciate this. Spain offered great exposure to it and of the depth of God's continuing devotion to me and my life. This I think of as his 'style'; a love that constantly seeks me for my own best interests.

It is greatly humbling and fantastically uplifting. It will take me a life time to fully digest.

Coming off the mountaintop-like experience of walking Spain, there was another sense of loss. The sadness I felt on both occasions as my walk concluded foretold of what was coming. I found it impossible to maintain the Spiritual high I had experienced. At the end of my walk I longed for home, yet wanted to somehow remain in 'Camino mode,' to continue walking indefinitely. The transition back to contemporary home life from that world was not straightforward, and I found I returned to a faith journey that continues at times to be a struggle. Balance I suppose always is. I still practice my religion, as its traditions and teachings are disciplines supporting my Spiritual growth. The difference is that I have an experience of what I believe to be deeper Spirituality, and understand I must lean more on that as relationship for it to grow fully. I know from Spain what relationship with God can feel like.

Having been to the mountaintop, I have a more grounded appreciation of my connection.

My experiences of a 21st century pilgrimage and the Camino de Santiago feel like they have moved me along the road of inner growth. Looking back on the last decade it seems there has been a direction and what looks like a kind of plan for me. I've simply needed to accept and walk each step along the way as it arrived. Starting in the fall of 2000 with the Robert Sibley newspaper series, or perhaps even before that, all the way to the present there has been a kind of building of one event on another leading me further along the path. I was drawn into the world of pilgrimage and gently my journey became public through no initiative on my part. I was kept there by workshops essentially instigated by others. My inner voice from 2003 brought me back six years later to walk again. To me, something larger has - is - developing over the years. There has been a kind of intertwining between circumstances of my life and events of the path that led back and forth to Spain. These no longer feel like individual stepping stones in my life. Something more is going on. I have followed a path, literal and figurative; allowing it to draw me in, I've come to accept God has his eye on the consequences.

I'm learning trust.

Deeply connected to this trust is the scriptural passage about the most important commandment; love God, love neighbor and love self. When I remember this passage, I realized I found this basic truth in an expression of my own making–pilgrimage separated the truly important of life from the merely necessary–while walking across Spain. My sense is that all the events I experienced, and many others I didn't write about, all belong to one of the three relationship spheres; love is the truly important. Obvious perhaps, but for me at least it requires constant reminding, and a clarity of the difference between love and the demanding realities of daily life. I found this love-based philosophy was described to me during my very first significant Camino encounter. It was from 2003 with Javier, the man who looked the part of an ancient prophet, the one who told me the journey is one of the heart.

I was on pilgrimage to feel.

A few of the people I came across during my Camino walks I've mentioned in these pages. There were others on both my walks with whom I had conversations about my faith journey, and the alignment of it with the beliefs of others. There was an amazing diversity of personal spiritual experiences and journeys. And yet, despite the differences, there was commonness to what each heart seemed to experience on pilgrimage. I chatted with a wide variety of folks from many different faith and non-faith disciplines, and as many or more different countries. Almost universally, all described an inner sense of being called to walk in Spain. With different words and different beliefs, with religious practice and without, the pilgrim's journey seemed internally similar for most. The walk touched something deep in each of us. It evoked a connection with that which might otherwise be unknowable. The similarity was perhaps most obvious in Santiago de Compostela, at the end of the pilgrimage trek during the daily noon mass for arriving walkers in the north western city. Regardless of faith, affiliation or belief, all sought out the mid day church service and the Pilgrims Blessing extended there. It was extraordinary to witness how the eyes of so many filled with tears of joy at the completion of their kilometers, and the sense of connection experienced in the Cathedral.

There was a spirit, a deeply experienced humanness, which was raised effortlessly to a level of great promise, and of Spirituality with the Divine.

The Camino de Santiago helped quiet the outside distractions, and allowed me to more fully appreciate the journey I'm on through my life. I realize I'm not alone on this road, and a quiet majority follow a similar route to the horizon, trying to discern faith and a relationship with God. The road I believe is unique to each of us, as unique as each distinctive personality. The distinctions affect relationships, beliefs, style and understanding, and possibly influence how many twists and turns are to be found along the way. I know for certain my uniqueness and my choices equal my changing character, my successes, my struggle, and my particular road.

Pilgrimage for me did separate the truly important from the merely necessary in my life. With changes to soften, slow and occasionally silence my world, I might be able to stay close to this pilgrim mode of understanding, of growing Spiritually. I need to keep the three relationship spheres front and centre, and let the merely necessary take only a minimum of my energy and attention. The changes I need are about gentleness of self, time for quiet, for meditation and for prayer, and more attention to the loves in my life. Perhaps it's summed up as gentleness of attitude. With love of God, self and others, and trust and acceptance, these changes will grow. I hope I will continue to let my heart lead, taking in as much as I can, the support and the challenges, and determine for myself what I believe, and how to follow the yellow arrows of life.

Whatever happens along the way, I'm a work in progress, and know I need to walk the road as I did in Spain; one day at a time.

Buen Camino

Appendix One
Camino 101–A Pre-Walk Camino de Santiago Planning Guide

For those who may wish to walk The Way of St. James, it is possible to plan a journey of the Camino using the websites listed in the next section. With these and other sites, information about what to plan can be found. For questions not answered by websites, a Camino forum is listed as a means to seek further detail. Over the years, many have successfully traveled to Spain following these sites. However, I found websites alone can be less than effective for reasons listed below. Based on my personal experiences and requests from my workshops, I created a pre-walk Guide called ***Camino Planning Guide*** for those who might prefer a more thorough approach.

Information gained from websites, and answers offered on Camino forum posts, aren't always clear. It is common to receive two or more different answers to the same question, simply based on the preference or opinion of the person posting the response. While there are circumstances where more than one response is appropriate, multiple answers without context are not always helpful. The real question when planning a walk of the Camino is "What information applies to me?" I have written **Camino Planning Guide** in response to this requirement.

Camino Planning Guide is divided into some two dozen sections (the table of contents is found below) covering everything from what to pack, how to train, how to get there, costs, language, safety, refugios and other considerations. (Packing checklists and important first hand tips are included.) Where feasible, each topic in this Planning Guide is covered under some or all of these headings:

- what the experts say to do
  –'The Expert Opinion'
- what I did on our trips
  –'My Experience'
- how well my experiences worked out
  –'20/20 Hindsight'
- the wider experience of others
  –'Walkers I Met'

'The Expert Opinion' is basically an amalgamation of all website information I have gathered over the years. '20/20 Hindsight' was written after my first walk, and identified things I would do differently if there was to be a second walk. **Camino Planning Guide** was updated with things I did do differently on my 2009 walk. Using this approach, there is sufficient context on each topic that you can determine what is going to emulate your preferences. For examples: connecting with others on both walks influenced my overnight stops; some people prefer walking in summer, while I prefer spring or fall; and some believe hiking boots are the best footwear, while others suggest sandals are the ideal. There are reasons why one option might be preferable to others. The background of these opinions and many others is explained, so you can choose the approach that best suits you.

The following is the Table of Contents from ***Camino Planning Guide:***

Topic:	Page #
Can You Do It?–Compare the Camino Experiences of the Author	3
The Origin of the Camino de Santiago	4
The Intention of the Guide	6
Key Points to Consider	7
Time of Year to Walk	8
How Long Does it Take?	9
Where Does It Start?	10
How Do I Get To the Camino?	12
How Demanding Is It to Walk 500 miles?	14
Safety	15
Statistics & the Credential Passport	16
Accommodations	18
Finding Your Way (along the trail)	20
Business Hours on the Camino	21
Daily Routine	23
How Much Does It Cost?	25
Language	27
Avoiding Health Issues	28

Training		30
What to Pack		34
Products We Purchased		38
Packing Checklists		39
Route Outline		
Conventional	- 33 Day Route	45
My 2003 Camino	- 30 Day Route	61
My 2009 Camino	- 28 Day Route	62
Pilgrim's Prayer		63
Philosophy & Spiritual Reflections		64
Frequently Asked Questions & Helpful Websites		71

There are a variety of books available on the market referred to as Camino Guides. Most are actually Maps and Accommodation Guides to carry on your walk, to help navigate the Camino when in Spain. Two of these are identified in the Websites listed and I recommend these as excellent for all travelers. The ***Camino Planning Guide*** by contrast is a 'pre-walk' Planning Guide, intended to help you plan your trip, train accordingly, and set expectations to fully enjoy your Camino. You should not expect to bring the ***Camino Planning Guide*** with you to Spain.

Camino Planning Guide can be purchased at the following website:

www.caminoplanning.com

Appendix Two
Camino Related Websites

- A popular Camino forum: http://www.caminodesantiago.me/board/

- 'Camino de Santiago Map - 2nd Edition' by Bethan Davies (and Ben Cole)–www.amazon.com–a small, sectional flip map for the backpack. Each section provides information such as the distance between towns, the route and any alternates, side interests, the amenities in the coming towns and villages, and elevation changes.

- The Confraternity of St. James–the UK organization that sells the 'Pilgrim Guide' to Spain - a listing of refugios and other accommodations–http://www.csj.org.uk

- 'American Pilgrims on the Camino' - http://www.americanpilgrims.com/ - US citizens can get a pilgrim's passport here

- 'Little Company of Pilgrims Canada' - http://www.santiago.ca–Canadian citizens can get a pilgrim's passport here

- A web listing of Refugios & Albergues along the Camino - http://www.caminosantiago.org/cpperegrino/cpalbergues/caminofrances.html
- Great Gallery of Camino Photos - *http://www.santiago-compostela.net/* - Click on 'Camino Frances' button, and then on buttons for Stages 1–30
- Local company (in Santiago de Compostela) offering miscellaneous support services (storing luggage up to 60 days, regional bus reservations, etc.) - http://www.caminotravelcenter.com
- A European weather site which provides access to historical weather patterns - *http://www.peterrobins.co.uk/camino/weather.html*
- General information site - http://www.santiago-today.com/
- Iberia Airlines: www.iberia.com
- Trains in France: http://www.voyages-sncf.com
- Trains in Spain: http://www.renfe.com/ingles/index.html
- Buses in Spain: http://www.alsa.es/44/Alsaindex.asp

Appendix Three
Questions for Discussion

What is your impression of coincidence, synchronicity and Divine Intervention?
- Describe one personal experience of each
- To which of these do you ascribe most events in your life–why?

What do you think of 21st century pilgrimage?
- Describe your impression of pilgrimage before reading this book
- How does your impression differ now? Why?
- Does pilgrimage, this one or any other, seem to call you?

Think about and describe a typical day, week and month of your life.
- What do you do each day that you would describe as truly important?
- What would you describe as merely necessary?
- Discuss your sense of balance between the two